THE ULTIMATE YOU!

CLARITY COACH MARLON GRIGSBY

*To my sons Cole, Marlon Jr. and Nathan.
May this book and my life be a guide for you
and your children's children to becoming
The Ultimate YOU!*

*To my beloved editor and mother, thank you
for everything!*

Feeling stuck in one or all areas of your life?

Are you wondering why you don't like your job. Why your family isn't where you would like them to be. Why you haven't started that business you have been talking about for years. Why you're going through the motions of life, but not truly happy. Why on the outside looking in people think your life is great, but that's far from the truth. Why your marriage or most significant relationship is shaky at best....

Imagine if...

I told you that you are dealing with these things because you don't have clarity in your life. What if I told you the biggest reason you have been struggling in one or all areas of your life and why your hopes and dreams have fallen short is because you have not become The ULTIMATE YOU!

Are you feeling like there is more inside of you to give and to do? Are you feeling comfortable in a lackluster and routine life? Are you not feeling challenged in your career? Are you making good money but still having to say "see the way my checking account is setup, I'm going to have to wait 2-3 days"? Are you dealing with relationship problems with your significant other or even contemplating divorce?

Over the past decade all this has happened to me. See, I have been stuck in just about every aspect of my life and I have done the hard and necessary work to get "unstuck". I know what works and what doesn't to get the clarity, understanding, direction and confidence back into your life. I know what it takes to feeling alive, present in life and happy again. I know what it means to stop BEING and to start LIVING.

Are you ready to become The ULTIMATE YOU?

All of your hopes, dreams and desires require you to be at your best, whether you realize it or not. This is why your family isn't where you would like them to be, why you haven't started that business, why your marriage is on the rocks and your most important relationships are just so-so. Trust me, I have been there and let me tell you… once I got clarity in my life, everything significantly changed for the better. This can all work for you. You can become the best version of yourself?

So, The Ultimate YOU! is a CATALYST for you to stop living your status quo life and being content in complacency, but to ELEVATE your life to the next level and to create the life of your dreams!

CLARITY IS THE THING THAT IS KEEPING YOU FROM EVERYTHING YOU EVER WANTED.

#LiveYourLegacy on your terms. Clarity is for those living under their potential to get unstuck and to transform every aspect of their life forever, no matter their current reality. Now that we have that out of the way let's dig in...

TABLE OF CONTENTS

INTRODUCTION TO THE ULTIMATE YOU!	9
GET A MASTER'S DEGREE IN YOU	13
FINDING YOUR PURPOSE & PASSION	19
DISCOVERING YOUR PERSONAL CORE VALUES	27
BREAKING THROUGH TO YOUR SUCCESS	31
WHAT IS A GREAT LIFE?	35
THE MOST IMPORTANT PERSON IN YOUR LIFE	41
MASTERING THE ART OF LETTING GO	45
MANIFESTING YOUR DREAMS	51
THE STORIES WE TELL OURSELVES	59
PERSPECTIVE (OR LIFE AS YOU KNOW IT)	63
STOPPING THE INNER CHATTER IN YOUR MIND	67
THE FORMATION OF YOUR BELIEF SYSTEM	71
PUTTING AN END TO YOUR LIMITING BELIEFS HOLDING YOU BACK	75
FREEDOM THROUGH FACING YOUR FEARS	81
CREATING A LIFE THEME	85
CASTING YOUR VISION	89

JOURNEY TO SELF-DISCOVERY	93
MANAGING STRESS IN A HEALTHY WAY	99
RELATIONSHIP RESTORATION	105
SUCCESS AND YOUR NEW DEFINITION	111
LIFE MASTERY	115
WORK-LIFE BALANCE	125
BECOMING THE ULTIMATE YOU!	131
ACHIEVING YOUR GOALS	135
OVERCOMING OBSTACLES IN YOUR WAY	141
SIMPLICITY AS A BLUEPRINT FOR SUCCESS	145
LIVE YOUR LEGACY	151
CONCLUSION	155

INTRODUCTION TO THE ULTIMATE YOU!

THE FACT THAT YOU are reading this book right now means you are someone who isn't willing to settle. You know you're meant for bigger things in life and you desperately crave a life of meaning and fulfillment. The issue is you are not sure what that is or how to get there. You're frustrated because your lack of direction has been holding you back. All you want is to meet your own expectations for your life, find your true happiness and to live a fulfilled life. Well, what if you knew exactly what you were meant to do and had all the tools to make your dream life a reality? I'm here to tell you it's possible. I have gone through a lot of ups and downs in my life and at various times I was really lost and I struggled with figuring out what to do with my life. I tried so many different things and many of them just didn't fit nor work for me like I would have hoped. I felt like I had to figure this out the slow way, by trial and error.

Tell me, does any of this sound familiar? You feel like something is missing in your life. You feel like you are just going through the motions of life and not truly living it. You are currently at a major crossroad and you need clarity before moving forward. You feel like you have been throwing your potential away just to get a paycheck. You are holding yourself back to start your business because you are scared to fail or maybe even scared to succeed. The things in your life just aren't in alignment with the person you desire to be. You know you have low confidence and it is affecting areas of your life. You're so confused and don't understand why you can't just be happy. You feel lost, confused or stuck in a specific area of life. You know what you want, but you are frustrated because you don't know how to get or achieve it.

Maybe you are unsure of how to connect the dots between your dreams and your reality. You are ready to take your life to the next level of achievement and excellence, however, you're sick of being stuck with no forward movement. You are ready to build a better mindset, better habits and a better life for yourself to become your ancestors' wildest dreams. You're finally ready to do something different in order to achieve the result you want.

Could you relate to any or all of what I just mentioned? If so, you're in the right place and I'm so glad you are reading this book right now? What if I told you that there was a way to overcome any obstacle standing between you and what you want, even if you feel you've tried everything before. What if I told you that the key to getting everything you ever wanted in life, and everything that you deserve, is already in you? The key is for you to become, The ULTIMATE YOU!

The foundation of the journey towards becoming The ULTIMATE YOU is taking the necessary steps to really understand yourself. It is about your journey towards continuous personal development and seeing life from a different perspective. It is about totally understanding exactly how you think, why you do things you do, your purpose and direction in life and the necessary steps to take your life, your happiness, your love, your money, your business, your career, all to the next level.

The ULTIMATE YOU is about knowing where you want to go and exactly how you're going to get there. It's like having the ability to go to Google Maps or Waze to type in your life's destination and it then gives you turn-by-turn directions on how to get there with incredible accuracy and extreme confidence. A life not being your best self is like getting in your car with no real destination in mind or trying to navigate yourself with no GPS and no map in a place that you are unfamiliar. Without this guidance you are just following your intuition and an old school compass to arrive at your destination. You would have very little confidence while you were driving. You would constantly second guess yourself and wonder if you were headed in the right direction or even on the right street. Many by default just go through life like this on cruise control, literally just wasting time and years until they figure life out for themselves and the destination that they are destined to go.

As you embark on this journey of clarity and of becoming The ULTIMATE YOU, your life will start to transform, problems and distractions will begin to shift away. The path to your purpose and your happiness will open up like the gates of heaven.

Throughout this process, you will notice a lot of things will begin to happen in your life and you will begin to change. This process is about being able to know, love and respect yourself for who you are and being able to express yourself to your fullest, to be authentic and unapologetically your true self. It's about having the confidence to express who you are. It's about not being afraid of what others may think of you. It's about being disciplined and being able to commit to your goals. It's about staying on your journey of self-discovery and self-empowerment. It's about having the right mental attitude to make decisions decisively and to take massive action on your life goals. It's about understanding your fears and taking the necessary steps to overcome them. It's about finding balance in your life, ensure that you are experiencing life and achieving things that are most important for you. It's about having true happiness in life. It's about creating your dream life and pushing towards your predetermined destiny.

Becoming The ULTIMATE YOU helps you achieve absolute success in whatever it is that you choose to pursue. When you start to truly understand and behave within this concept that we will go through, you will start to see your success accelerate exponentially through every aspect of your life.

Trust me. If it is possible for me, it's 100% possible for you, too! I'm not special. I'm just a person who has learned how to get myself unstuck and moving towards my dreams and goals like never before. Always remember, no one is better at being you, than you. So make sure you are becoming, The ULTIMATE YOU!

GET A MASTER'S DEGREE IN YOU

RIGHT NOW WE ARE discussing a better understanding of you. We all have spent a large percentage of our lives in school. Some 16+ years of learning new things that make you brighter, smarter and more prepared for a career and the workforce. While all this education is important, it has had very little effect on your everyday life, outside of what type of profession you were going to choose. Don't get me wrong, your career choice is very important, mainly because it will affect your money, your lifestyle and happiness tremendously. Outside of that though what good is all this personal academic knowledge if you really don't know who you truly are? Do you know your personal core values? Your internal belief system? Your strengths, talents and giftings? Do you know your passions in life? If you answered no or I don't know to these questions, it's very easy to become unhappy in your life and in your career. While you love earning a good income, if you hate the work you do, the benefits of a high income will not make you happy in the long run.

When you really get to know yourself for who you are, it affects every aspect of your life: your family relationships, your love life, your friendships, your career, your motivation, your money, your business if you have one, your home life and even your spirituality. You name it, it's affected by how well you know or don't know yourself. Ralph Ellison is quoted saying, "When I discover who I am, I'll be free." We are living in an age where you can study and learn anything you want in a moments notice.

I remember when I was remodeling my home, 50% of the things I wanted to do I had no idea how to do, but I was able to learn by watching DIY YouTube videos that showed me how to do these things. There are so many content providers out there, from the professional to the novice, from big corporations to individuals, from outstanding content to garbage, but the point is that the know-how is there, if you take the time to look for it. I remember learning how to put up canned lights, changing out electrical outlets, putting new faucets in, adding trendy accent walls and many other things all from researching online. This means a lot as I'm more like a Phil Dunphy from Modern Family or a Tim "The Tool Man" Taylor than I'm a Bob the Builder. When I'm not learning how to remodel, I'm learning how to do basic home and car repairs when something breaks. The first thing I do is to pull out my phone and type in "how do I fix... whatever my issue is". When I have something going on with my body, the first thing I do is try to self-diagnosis myself online. I'm sure this really bothers many medical professionals when patients diagnosis themselves based off what they learned from the Internet, because as we know not everything is accurate out there, but I hope they appreciate our effort to aide in the process.

So let's take it down to even the simplest form of knowledge gathering. I'm notorious for when I go to a new restaurant, before I do anything, including looking at the menu, I go to Yelp, look at the reviews and the customer pictures of actual entrees, so I know if this place is going to be good and what entrees stand out for me to order. I even do this for places I frequent, when I want to try something different. Let's talk about vacations. Before deciding where I want to go, I do all types of research from Trip Advisor to Lonely Planet and I get a good sense if this is somewhere I want to go, what to do while I'm there, places of interest in the vicinity and, of course, good places to eat.

We live in an age where knowledge is power and you can learn anything you want just by a quick search on your phone. With all that being said, isn't it about time that you take the time to learn about yourself? Isn't it time for you to take the opportunity to invest into yourself. It's fine for you to get to know who you really are outside of your profession or personal responsibilities. By picking up this book and even going a step further and going through The ULTIMATE YOU clarity course, that you can find at www.marlongrigsby.com, you will be getting an equivalent of a master's degree with a specialization in YOU! This single decision has the greatest potential to affect your long-term happiness and success more than you could ever, ever know.

The famous author Debbie Ford said, "Self-awareness is the ability to take an honest look at your life without any attachment to it being right or wrong, good or bad." Socrates said, "The unexamined life is not worth living."

By knowing yourself you get an invaluable understanding of your personality, behaviors, habits, emotional reactions, motivations and thought processes. By being self-aware, you make better choices in all aspects of your life, both personally and professionally.

It's kind of like the red and blue pill in the Matrix. When Morpheus offers Neo a choice between the two pills. He said, "After this, there is no turning back. You take the blue pill - the story ends, you wake up in your bed and believe whatever you want to believe. You take the red pill - you stay in Wonderland, and I show you how deep the rabbit hole goes. Remember: all I'm offering is the truth."

Your life and a life being self-aware is like taking the red pill. No one knows you better than you, so bypass your well-intentioned friends and family that offer you advice on your life. Potentially skip the therapy and counseling sessions. All the answers you're seeking are already within you and by you taking the red life clarity pill, all you need to know will be brought to your consciousness.

Tennis legend Billie Jean King said, "I think self-awareness is probably the most important thing towards being a champion." Imagine the confidence you'll feel when you finally know who you are, what you want and why you want it. You will learn to trust that inner you that you previously overlooked and ignored. That you that has been buried deep inside of your shattered dreams, lost ambitions, unmet expectations and limiting beliefs. So I implore you, stay on course and don't get unplugged from the Matrix, as this is necessary towards you becoming all you've ever dreamed of and more!

Have you ever thought to yourself, who am I really? Everyone says that you should just "be yourself", but what does that even mean? What does being yourself really feel like? Do you know who you are outside of your roles and responsibilities in life? Outside of your occupation, who are you? What do you stand for? Outside of being a parent, who are you? Outside of being a spouse or someone's Boo or Bae, who are you?

The only way to know how to be yourself, is to understand who you are at your deepest, most core level. Who you are is not your job, it's not your name, nor any of the labels that have been put on you through the years. Who you are is underneath all of that.

I remember the day that I was challenged by this. Someone asked me who I was and I proceeded to tell them what I did for a living. Then they said no. Who are you? Then I told them that I'm a father, a husband, where I was from, where I worked and what part of town I lived. They again said no, is THAT really who you are? My answer described my relationship to my family and where I spent most of my time to bring in an income. While this does give me some insight into my life, it tells very little about who I am for real.

Are you at a place where I was? Where you truly don't know who you are. For me, it was very frustrating to come up with an authentic answer, so I knew I had to explore it. To be honest, it took some time. I walked around for years, no decades, lost to who I truly was and I didn't even realize it. I had no identity outside my relationships with my family and my career.

Discovering who you are and what you want out of life will help you live a life where you feel fulfilled every day. If you let your life pass you by without discovering these things, then you are just going through the motions, literally sleepwalking through life. Your life has meaning. It has a very unique purpose. You have gifts and talents buried deep inside of you that need to be shared with the world.

One key to discovering who you really are starts with getting quiet, being still and listening for the answers to those deep questions. Let's be honest, we live in a very noisy and busy world. Sometimes even the most intential people fill up their lives with busyness and distractions to numb out the pain and frustrations of an unfulfilled life. Truth be told, you have probably been compromising who you really are and not living up to your full potential for a very long time now and that's partly why you are reading this book. Don't be ashamed or upset about it, half the battle is knowing. Today is a new day and the perfect day for change.

Socrates once said, "To know thyself is the beginning of wisdom". Knowing who you really are is the secret sauce to self-understanding, true love, financial prosperity, career success, happiness and so many other great things in your life. Happiness will come when you are able to express who you are and not care about other's perceptions or thoughts about you because you are being true to your authentic self.

When your actions are in accordance with your feelings and values, you will experience less internal conflicts. Without this internal battle going on inside of you, this leads to better overall decision-making in your life. When you know yourself, you are able to make better choices, from the small seemingly insignificant decisions like what should I wear today, to big important vital decisions like which job am I going to take, or colossal decisions like should I stay at my job, should I marry this person or should I stay in this relationship. When you know who you are, you'll have the internal guidelines to solve some of life's big and small problems with ease.

During this process of self-discovery you will learn your values and other tools which will also serve as motivation towards your goals. You will learn your interests, your temperament and your strengths. I do want to caution you that being true to the core of who you are, is actually much harder than it looks. It's hard to remain true to who you really are because not only are you constantly changing and evolving, but those around you in your friends, family, your job and even what today's culture values usually conflicts with what's deep down inside of you. I don't want you to worry about it. By the end of this book you will know the principles and concepts used for true self-discovery. If you go a step further and decide to take The ULTIMATE YOU self-discovery immersion and clarity course you will be even more solid on knowing who you really are for real and start living the life of your dreams with intentionality and purpose.

FINDING YOUR PURPOSE & PASSION

Sometimes the combination of a successful career, a loving family and a strong social network may seem like the recipe for a perfect life. However, even if you had all of those boxes checked in your life, it may feel like something is missing. Most likely that is why you are reading this book now. You probably have everything you need for a great life, but it still feels like there's more out there for you. This is normal, so don't worry.

Let's take an initial look at discovering your life's purpose. There are many reasons why you may not know your life purpose currently and that's okay. Sometimes it's because the world's problems seem way too big and you feel way too small, to make an impact. It might just be that you are just exhausted from normal life and don't know where you'll find the energy to fight for what really matters to you as a life purpose. Many think the cause that's near and dear to their hearts and what they are passionate about is too small, while others are on the opposite spectrum and think their cause is way too big to make a difference. It doesn't matter the size of your cause, but the nature and the impact is what you need to keep in mind.

The famous John D. Rockefeller said, "Singleness of purpose is one of the chief essentials for success in life, no matter what may be one's aim."

If you want to experience inner peace and ultimate fulfillment, it's critical that you learn how to find your passion and life purpose. Without a life purpose as the compass to guide you, your goals and action plans most likely will not fulfill you.

Identifying, acknowledging and honoring this purpose is perhaps the most important action successful people take on a continual basis. They take the time to understand what they're here to do and then they pursue that with extreme passion and enthusiasm.

For some, your purpose and passion in life is obvious and clear. You were born with a set of talents and through persistent practice, you developed your talents into skills and ended up taking them with you to South Beach. For some, you have innate natural talents that are very clear indicators of your passion like art or writing. For some like me, it's not as easy to identify a passion. You may even have asked yourself at one point or another in your adult life, "What do I want to be when I grow up?"

So here's the thing about people, we love what we're good at. It's the reason why someone finds themselves working the same career for twenty or thirty years, even if it isn't something they necessarily enjoy doing. This is because people can easily be creatures of habit and the risk of leaving and trying something else, something you might not be as good at, is too high of a risk to take, so you decide to play it safe and stay in your comfort zone.

We also love when we're proficient. As a result, we cultivate skills that are more socially acceptable or that people around us encourage us to nurture, so much so that eventually, they become our primary skill sets. Even if we had originally wanted or dreamed of doing something different with our lives, we struggle to move in that direction because those skills are not as easily cultivated and it takes time to work and develop them into strengths. Also, there is often not an immediate pay off, nor is there often encouragment by those that are closest to us. Usually big shifts like this are met with criticism, skepticism or half-hearted support from a distance. So when we operate like this, it's kind of our little secret until we have success or achievement, then we want to proudly shout from the rooftops. You know that business you always wanted to start, that new career or job you always wanted, that adventure you always want to conquer that stays in your maybe one-day goals. That's really a place goals go to be lost forever, but never forgotten.

Let's think about this practically. You may work eight hours a day doing something you never wanted to do or no longer want as your primary job. So much time has gone by that you have become incredibly proficient and would feel literally insecure about having to learn a new skill set and doing something different.

Maya Angelou once said, "There is no greater agony than bearing an untold story inside you."

So let's talk about some ways to start exploring your life purpose, your passion and to start tapping into that untold story inside of you. You were born with a deep and meaningful purpose that you have to discover. Your purpose is not something you need to make up, it's already there. You have to uncover it in order to create the life you want for the future. You may be asking why am I having so much trouble finding out what I'm passionate about? Anyone who knows me personally, knows I'm a huge Pittsburgh Steelers, The Ohio State football and a Lebron James fan. However, this is not what I'm talking about. Your favorite sports team or your favorite social platform may be interests that you like and are highly invested in, but not what you are passionate about. I'm talking about passion in the most broadest sense like an interest that goes beyond yourself. In our society today, many people are hurting, disinterested or disconnected because they are not chasing their passion. I know this to be true because I was this way myself for a long time.

Listen, you need to find your passion and your secret sauce to be truly happy in life. One of the most interesting things about finding your purpose is that no one else can find this for you. Maybe your parents or a mentor have tried to give you insight they see for you and maybe those suggestions worked. Even as your coach, I can't give you the answers. What I can give you is the clarity from your past, the truth of your present life and the peace of mind to lead you to figuring this out for yourself.

Ultimately, success in life depends on you leading your life into the direction that you want to go. The terminology I like to use is to "live your legacy". So what can you do? You can start by slowing your life down a bit. Give yourself a break from multitasking. Take a deep breath and relax. Life doesn't become more meaningful if you simply fill it up with more tasks, more meetings and more busyness. Try doing more with less and allow yourself to appreciate completing something with excellence. Stop distracting yourself. Pay attention to what's going on around you. Passion happens when you are like a child and are feeling playful and exuberant. When you're in touch with your passion, when you're doing something just because you love it, not because you're especially good at it, make a lot of money doing it nor because other people tell you that you should be doing it. When you are in touch with your passion, this is the moment you start living your life for real.

When you pursue your passion, you feel good about it. I'm a true advocate of encouraging people to find time for themselves as a means to greater happiness overall. Life just feels better when you have things in your day that you want to do, no matter how simple or difficult, it's just better. You know those moments where time almost stands still. The more time you can spend in that zone, the better life feels as a whole and the happier you will be.

In today's society your phone is an extension of you and you are always connected and in tune to what's going on. What is it that you are doing when you put your phone down and forget to look at it for an extended period of time? What things did you love to do as a kid that you may not be doing any longer? What feels like active relaxation and brings peace into your life, whether it's hard work or not? What fires you up and gets you excited from your core? What would you do if money didn't matter? If you can answer these questions, they will help you identify what you're passionate about.

I get it, we're all very busy. Whether you're juggling a demanding career, family life or both, it's very possbile you feel as if there is no way you can fit anything more into your schedule. However, when you say you don't have time, what you're really saying is, you are not a priority to yourself. While there are definitely moments in which you legitimately don't have time to spare, I bet you can find a little time if you knew how important it was to your ultimate happiness.

Working on yourself makes you the best possible person not only for you, but for others connected to you. Whether you engage in something personal or professional, self-improvement is a win-win scenario. If you open yourself up to new experiences by gradually stepping outside your comfort zone, you can find the things that truly make you happy. Whether those things become hobbies or your life's work, pursuing your passions can give you a renewed sense of meaning and accomplishment.

Life is dynamic and so are your interests. You might love things in certain seasons of life but not so much in other times. If you look at the actual things you love to do as a guide to finding your passion themes, you'll notice they can evolve into some pretty awesome moments, opportunities or even a career you didn't even know existed. Actually, did you know the more time you spend working on something, the more invested you become to it? Any interest that you can hone in on and can turn into a passion. Sometimes you have to pursue something before you know how deep your interest runs in it. When in doubt, follow your curiosity and see where it takes you. Oprah says, "There is no greater gift you can give or receive than to honor your calling. It's why you were born. And how you become most truly alive."

I remember the first time I ran a 5K race which is 3.1 miles long. I couldn't believe it, that was monumental for me because I was never a long distance runner. So once I completed it, I decided to just do it again and again until I worked my way up to a full 26.2 mile marathon. The love for running and the results to my body that I gained from it began with one small 5K race. If you listen closely to the voices inside your head, they'll guide you in the right direction towards your passion. By the way you can have multiple passions, one may be stronger than another or one may have more time granted to it by you, but you can definitely have more than one and that's okay.

For me, my love for travel turned into something that I would have never dreamed. I have been to more than 20+ countries and counting and to 4 of the 7 continents. This passion has turned me into creating travel experiences for others in group travel. My love for running, fitness and how it all affects my body turned into running a marathon and being in probably the best shape of my life. My combined love for life and self-development turned into this book and impacting other's lives, not just my own, through clarity coaching.

I could go on about my own story, but I want you to have your own. I want you to wake up feeling excited because you're doing at least one thing a day that gets you out of your own head and going. What's the one thing that makes you forget Instagram even exists? What's the one thing that just fills your cup.

Taking action to discover, practice and evolve your passions isn't going to be easy. It takes time, energy, being open to new things and a whole lot of love and respect for yourself. It often required me to get really vulnerable and to do things alone. Now, I actually love doing the things I love either by myself or with others, because I love it. Being able to share something you love with others is always the icing on the cake. Creating experiences to remember and establishing life bonds with others is more than just sharing your passion, you are sharing and doing life together. The most enlightening and reassuring thing that I've discovered is that the more I show the world who I am, the more amazing things, opportunities and people come back to me. That's an awesome feeling to have and I want you to feel it for yourself.

Revaluating and Assessing Your Life

When your life takes an unexpected sideways turn, it's easy to make a hasty ill-advised decision and end up regretting it later. The need to revaluate your life can come from a lot of different scenarios. Perhaps you've just lost your job or been made redundant, maybe a long-term relationship has ended or maybe you've just found yourself depressed, unsatisfied or antsy with your current life situation.

Revaluating your life is usually the first step to making a major change. A life audit is a fundamental part of assessing how far you've come, where you want to go, what you should stop doing and everything you should keep doing to become a better version of yourself as you pursue your purpose and passion. It's a self-reflection exercise. An audit will leave you with the clarity and space that you need to "do you" at the ultimate level.

When you audit your life, performance improves. No matter how accomplished or happy you currently are, you have specific areas of your life that could use some improvement or a different focus to get you back on track. Think about your health, for instance. Are you in a peak state of health, feeling energetic and full of vitality? If so, congratulations! Now move on to another area, such as personal finance. Are you on the right track to achieve financial freedom? What about your career? Does your job feel like a job, something you go to every day to earn income or is it more of a mission, something you would do even if you weren't getting paid for it?

The Wheel of Life exercise is a way to take a good, hard look at each facet of your life and rate its relative quality level, so you can uncover which areas need more attention than others. Consider each area like a spoke of a wheel. When one of the spokes is shorter than the others, it can throw the whole wheel off balance. By getting this "helicopter" view of your life, you can identify where you are excelling and where there is room for improvement. You can discover where the gaps are between where you are and where you want to be. To be able to create your dream life, you must first create a strategic map of where you are today and where you desire to be tomorrow.

Have you ever asked yourself, "What can I do to improve myself and my life?" Many people have asked themselves this question at some point in their lives as part of their personal development. Life is a journey and sometimes you can get stuck in the same position for a long time or you may even get lost in it like a maze as you hit one dead end after another.

When you are at a place of frustration or lack of progress in your personal or professional life, this is when you need to stop and take the time to analyze your life. You need to look at where you are, where you want to go and how you intend to get there. One of the best ways to do this is by writing and using a strategic plan for your life.

In writing a strategic plan, you begin by assessing your current situation or where you are now. Various tools can be used to do this, but one of the best tools is a S.W.O.C. analysis, which is an acronym for strengths, weaknesses, opportunities and challenges. Strengths and weaknesses are considered internal factors, most of which are within your control. Opportunities and challenges are considered external factors, most of which are outside your control. Your strengths and opportunities are things you can use to help improve your life. Your weaknesses and challenges are things you need to improve and manage. A S.W.O.C. analysis helps you see what is happening and how you can make changes to have a better life overall. Under weaknesses, list your areas for improvement. We all have areas for improvement. If you are not sure what areas you need to improve, ask someone who you believe will tell you the truth. Sometimes it is easier to identify areas of improvement in others than it is to identify them in yourself. You can ask that person to help you identify your strengths, as well as, your areas for improvement. As you do your S.W.O.C., focus on the major areas for improvement and those that will help you live a better life. Under opportunities, list the things you think you can do to improve your life, your options and things you believe are possible for you. Under challenges, list some of the major difficulties you are experiencing, the obstacles you face and any major threats to your life's happiness.

After identifying your strengths, weaknesses, opportunities and challenges, ask yourself the following questions:

1. How can I use my strengths to help myself, serve others and live a better life?
2. Which of my weaknesses do I need to improve and how can I improve them?
3. What opportunities can I explore to improve myself and my life?
4. What can I do about the challenges I face?

DISCOVERING YOUR PERSONAL CORE VALUES

HAVE YOU EVER ASKED yourself what the real influences of your decisions are? Why you prefer one situation over another? For instance, why do you prefer being an employee over being an entreprenuer or vice versa? Why do you live where you live? Why you are with the person you are in a relationship with? It's just because of your circumstances, because real decisions were not involved with all of these scenarios. So why are you making these decisions?

The answer lies at the core of your character and it's what defines you as a person and it is known as your personal value system.

Simply put, values set you clear on the things that are important to you. Values are the things you believe are important in your life and your work. They usually determine your priorities and they are your yardstick for measuring whether your life is turning out the way you want it to or not. Together, they make up your why. Understanding your values can also help you get clear on what's not working in your life, so that you can create guardrails for your future decisions and end up somewhere better aligned with who you are. When you live according to your values, you feel a sense of ease and direction in your choices. Conversely, you can often feel out of whack when you make decisions that are not aligned with your values. Bottom line, decision-making is very hard when you can't clearly articulate your values.

Your values come from a variety of sources like your family, peers, work, education, significant life events, religion, music, culture, historical events and any other pivotal foundational things from your life. Values are formed starting in early childhood and are usually enforced and further developed throughout your life. Personal values are generally operating in the background of your life. They influence everything you do, but usually it does so on auto-pilot and in your subconscious. You just know intuitively what you like and make decisions accordingly, based off your values.

It is necessary to know and understand your personal values. Knowing your personal values gives you clarity, builds your self-awareness and acts like a guide for you through life. It also makes decision making much easier. Knowing your negative values, those from which you try to keep away from, are also very helpful. When you are clearly aware of your value hierarchy you can consciously check situations against your personal value-system. Not only is decision making easier but it will also be easier to keep your balance in life knowing your core values.

I'm telling you, the most important thing you can do for your personal success today is to know your core values, use them to guide you to success, to your destiny and to your purpose. Knowing your core values is important because when you need to choose or decide something later, you can do so easily by determining if the choice lines up with your true values. A life lined up with personal core values is a life well-lived and a purpose-filled life.

So just what are values? Values define what is important to you throughout many different situations. They develop based on your subjective world view. Every individual has a different world view and their own mix of values with their own hierarchy. For some, personal freedom is important. For others security, social justice or preserving nature is important.

Values simply put, are a part of you. They highlight what you stand for and represent your unique individual essence. Values guide your behavior and provide you with your own personal code of conduct. When you honor your personal core values consistently, you begin to experience fulfillment through all areas of life.

When you don't, you are incongruent and are more likely to escape into bad habits and regress into childish behaviors to try to uplift yourself. Most people don't know their true core values. They don't understand what's most important to them. Instead, they focus on what society, culture and media values and what gets the most "likes".

Try it right now, can you articulate your top 5 to 10 core values that are most important to you? Without undergoing a discovery process, it's challenging to identify your personal core values. It's easy to speculate and idealize what they should be, but knowing and accepting what you truly value to the core of your being takes time, effort and reflection to do so. If you don't know or are unsure, complete a core value worksheet to gain some clarity in this area.

BREAKING THROUGH TO YOUR SUCCESS

WHAT IS SUCCESS? NOT my success, not your company's success, but what's your success? Only you know what success means for you. When we break this down, I go by a strategy called the "IT" Methodology for success breakthroughs. There are several IT's in the IT Methodology, including Dream IT, Believe IT, See IT, Tell IT, Plan IT, Work IT and Enjoy IT.

When you are breaking through to your success you first need to Dream IT. Everything begins in the heart and the mind. Every great achievement and success began in the mind of one person including yours. They dared to dream, to believe that it was possible. You, as well, need to take some time to allow yourself to ask "What if?" and think BIG. Dream of the possibilities for yourself, your family and for others. If you had a dream that you let stall and fade into the sunset, reignite that dream! Fan the flames. Life is too short to let it go and dwindle away.

Once you Dream IT, you better Believe IT! If you don't believe it, no one else will believe it for you either. You must be able to say that if certain things take place, if others help, if I work hard enough, though it is a big dream, it can still be done.

Once you Believe IT can and will happen you have to See IT. Those that have achieved great success have always seen it before they achieved it. They picture themselves running their business, eradicating a need in society, doing what they are passionate about. Steph Curry pictures the ball going through the hoop before he shoots it, Tiger Woods sees the ball going in the hole before he putts. Actors see themselves stepping into the character they are playing well before they say lights, camera, action.

Now that you See IT, you need to Tell IT. One reason many dreams never go anywhere is because the dreamer, yep that's you, keeps it all to themself. It is a quiet dream that only lives inside of your mind. You don't share it, because what if it doesn't happen? What if your dream is actually kind of silly to others? What if it is too outlandish and too BIG and others doubt you? The one who wants to achieve success must tell their dreams of success to many people before the success can happen. One reason is, as you continually tell it, you begin to believe it more and more in your subconscious. If you are talking about it then it must be possible, right? Another reason is that talking to others holds you accountable. When you tell others, it creates a level of urgency for you to actually start doing it, so you don't look foolish. I remember telling people that I was going to go sky diving for the first time, even though I was afraid of heights. I told people because I thought about this principle, that I need to tell others to keep me accountable to what I said I was going to do. I did that because I knew for every person I told the less likely I was to back out at the last minute. I remember writing this book, I told no one, because I was not a "writer" and who was going to buy a book about living their legacy and creating their best life? Needless to say, my progress on the writing process was slow and difficult. However, once I applied the "IT" Methodology, writing became a lot easier as I was not just writing aimlessly. I saw the outcome. I saw people's lives being changed forever. I saw those taking these words and applying it to their everyday lives for a lasting impact.

Okay, so once you Tell IT, you better Plan IT. Every successful achieved dream must take the form of a plan. Your dream won't just happen as you sit there and visualize it, pray for it and hope for the best. You need to sit down on a regular basis and plan out your strategy for achieving this dream of yours. Think through all of the details. Break the whole plan down into small, workable parts. Then set a timeframe for accomplishing each task on your success plan.

Perfecto! You have the plan, so guess what you are going to do now? You got to Work IT! The successful are usually the hardest workers. While the rest of the world is sitting on their sofas watching TV or shooting the breeze, achievers are working on their goal, they're grinding, hustling and striving for success and achieving their dream, no matter the costs.

Final step after you worked hard and sacrificed a lot to get it, you now have to sit back, smell the roses and bask in glory as you Enjoy IT. If your breakthrough was to run a marathon, fix a broken relationship, get a new job, start a business, make more money, find the love of your life, lose so many pounds of weight, whatever it is once you achieve it, celebrate and Enjoy IT! It took a lot of work to achieve it so when you have reached your goal be sure to take it all in. In fact, you need to also enjoy the process and the journey to get there as well. These are going to be the stories that make up who you are and what you are made of as you breakthrough to your success. Along the way give yourself some rewards for achieving major milestones to keep you encouraged as you measure your progress and you see how much you have accomplished thus far. Give yourself a huge reward when you get to that finish line of reaching your goal because you deserve it. Once you are finished with your first breakthrough, the process gets easier and easier, so the next thing to do is to repeat it on something else that's going to light a fire under your passion and make you even more successful in another life area.

WHAT IS A GREAT LIFE?

WHAT IS A GREAT life? Personally, my answer now is different than it would have been 30, 20, 10 or even 5 years ago. Your definition of a great life probably changes as you go into different seasons of life. My belief now is that there is no one-size-fits-all answer as greatness is different for everyone. I think a "great life" has similar elements amongst most people, but how you achieve it, live it and appreciate it are all totally unique.

Living a great life could mean different things to different people. Generally speaking, it means a life that brings you happiness and peace. Most people get busy in their lives and tend to forget the little moments that lead to a great life. You know those moments that have the power to make your life magical. For some living a great life would seem like you need to live your big dreams that require you to put in a lot of time and effort. However, living a great life is not about money and not about the big things. It is about the small manageable things which are within reach for everyone. For some it's to provide for and make sure their children have every possibility for success. For others it may be to climb to the top of the corporate ladder. For others it may be to serve as many people as possible, to travel and experience the world, to love unapologetically. Each person's definition of greatness is different and that's the way it should be.

It is not difficult to live a fulfilling life, provided you are ready to change yourself and change your mindset. People in general, always want more, which is okay, if it is within reason. Suppose you own a nice condo, but you want a house after a while, and once you get that, then you would want a bigger house. Your desires and demands keep increasing and changing as you live. You are never really content with what you have and that perhaps is literally just human nature or at least societal norms as we get bombarded with images of other's definitions of wants, desires and our need for "likes". As a result, to achieve all this, people are urged to work harder and earn more money. This results in leading busy and more stressful lives as opposed to simple and stress free lives.

When this natural progression happens, people don't have time to do things that really matter. They especially do not have time for themselves. They don't have time to do things they like to do, such as being outdoors or spending time with their family and friends. Actually, you really need very little to lead a great life. If you look around yourself, no matter who you are, you already have enough, such as consumer goods, money or other such things.

I remember being on a mission trip years ago in Rwanda. We were in the very rural parts of the country. People were living in huts made out of dirt, mud and trees. They seemingly had very little, but after I got to know them, they were so very rich. Their hearts were full of love, acceptance, respect, nurturing spirits and contentness. They were a community full of forgiveness despite the geneocide that happened decades prior. Their hearts were so wide open and they lacked nothing. How is it that these people were so happy and we who seemingly have everything are seemingly never content?

See, you want more because the desire to have more does not end. However, you need to decide what is more important to you to have a great life. Is it the materialistic things to make you feel important or living an amazing and peaceful life regardless of what you have?

WHAT IS A GREAT LIFE?

I was out with some friends for dinner a while ago and I had a real authentic conversation about what exactly it means to "live a great life". It turned out that we all had somewhat different views on what "a great life" actually is. For one person at the table, it meant that he could finally start his own business and be an entrepreneur, make lots of money and set his own hours. For another it was to not have to want for anything any longer. If she wanted to take a vacation she could. If she wanted to quit her job, pay for her kids college education or buy a new car, she could without having to think twice about it. For another it was good health. To be able to live a long life, without the personal ailings that they were currently dealing with. For me, I thought about it for a bit and said that, a great life is one filled with peace, plain and simple. Meaning that there were minimal ongoing things that worried me. No drama, no financial worries, authentic love, true friendships and no major incidents that could rock my proverbial world.

From our conversation most ideas around living a great life centered around a few core ideas. A great life involves the removal of ongoing stress. A great life involves being a good person to others and being around others that recipricate that back to you. A great life involves having sufficient financial resources to have financial freedom and various options in life. A great life involves having something worthwhile to do with your time, from work to family and friends. A great life also involves being personally healthy.

While the ideas of what made up this great life varied far and wide, they almost always included those elements in some way, shape, or form. Low stress. Good people around you. Being good yourself. Having sufficient resources for things you want to do. Being physically and mentally healthy. Having something meaningful and engaging to do with your time. Almost every concept of the great life either relied on those things or were variations of them.

To reconnect with your great life there are several things you need to start or continue to do. You should stop working so hard and slow down your pace. Instead, start scheduling some leisure or "me" time. This should be a constant reminder for us all, me incuded.

You must spend time with your parents, children, family and friends. Let go of negative friendships and those who pull you down to a place of uneasiness or lack of peace. You must forgive those who have hurt you in the past. Face it and accept the pain and hurt, but then you need to let it go, as you can't change the past and you certainly shouldn't be living in it. This is a big way you heal yourself. Once you do that, you will see wonderful things entering into your life that you have been blind to before, because you have been singing woe is me and constantly complaining, you will never make it too far in life playing the victim role.

You must travel near and far visiting different places that will widen your horizons. Meet new people, make new contacts and just be present as you enjoy life. You must focus on your life's passions. You must help and be of service to others, as that ultimately will bring you happiness and satisfaction. You must remain positive even when life has its down moments. The year 2020 was a challenging one for the whole world, no matter how desperately we all just wanted to restart the year or fast forward past it, we had to sit in it, reflect and look for the positive things, even if they were few and far between. Also, don't try to be perfect. You are reading this book because you are an over-achiever, but don't try to be perfect. Perfection is an impossible never ending target that could keep you in a place of not being content with yourself striving for perfection which is an impossible goal.

You should also lead a healthy lifestyle. You are what you eat, so eat clean and healthy food. Look after yourself by taking time to exercise and sleep well. Many in the basketball world are in awe of how LeBron James can have such a long and remarkable career. His secret is that he really takes care of himself. It's reported that he invests about a million dollars a year into his body and keeping it in impeccable condition. While you might not be able to invest a million dollars a year into protecting your body, your career probably doesn't demand as much physically either, but you get the point. Remember, a tired mind is unhappy and inefficient.

You also need to learn to enjoy life's moments. Take out time to appreciate the simple pleasures in life. There are so many good things and simple pleasures, take them in, enjoy them and value them. Never stop learning. Never stop laughing and having things to make you laugh. Love someone more than you think you can. Love your family and spend time with them because they are the people who matter most. A life unloved isn't much of a life at all.

Accept and adapt to change easily. When you come across failures, look to the positive aspect of each. Each failure teaches you something in return and makes you stronger, wiser and propels you towards success.

Learn to give. There is great joy in giving. The more you give, the more you receive. Even if you don't get back anything in return, at least you know you have done a good deed. Giving isn't always monetary, it could be giving of your time, your talents or your treasures.

Finally, just learn to be yourself! You are you and no one else, so don't try to copy someone to please others or yourself. You don't have to do that, nor will you be able to do it for long. Just be who you are unapologetically and people will love you for it. You will also get to weed out who your real friends are from the superficial ones this way.

I would say that living a great life is being happy and content with all that you are blessed to have. Yes, pursue your dreams, of course, don't stop doing that, but keep enjoying the special moments and people in your life. I hope you now have a new perspective on what a GREAT life is and are ready to start living a more meaningful one. Remember, it is your life, so make it a great one!

So I ask you. What does a great life mean to you?

THE MOST IMPORTANT PERSON IN YOUR LIFE

It's Time You Realize that YOU are the most important person in your life. When you find value in yourself your whole world will change. The thing is, you are meant to be a bird that can fly free and explore the world, not one that is held back and limited by a cage. Many of you limit your lives like you are in a proverbial cage. Caged in by time, life's circumstances, finances, work and family responsibilities. When you learn to look in the mirror you should see wings that need to be spread to fly, not chained down or subdued. You have to move on from whatever it is that is holding you back. You have to move on from whatever has been weighing you down and dust your shoulders off as you learn to fly free again. For some, this will be very difficult as you haven't done so since you were a child. You know that innocent age where you dreamed and there weren't any limits to your imagination. That's the time you need to get back to because you are the real M.V.P. here.

Plain and simple, you cannot allow other people to hold you back by having more power over your life than you do yourself. So often people lower themselves to the standards that others hold them to. When you place others limiting beliefs about you on you, allowing their words to literally smother your dreams, your passions and your joy. I've done it, you've done it and so has everyone else to some degree. When you give the key to your inner-being to others, ask yourself are they deserving of it. Honestly, the only person who deserves to hold the key to your life is you, not your parent, your spouse, your sibling or anyone else. It's all you!

So here's the deal, your self-worth is not determined by another person's opinion of you. You are not defined by the messed up life situation you're in, but rather your mental attitude and the tools you use to fix whatever is broken in your life. It's like having Iyanla Vanzant Fix Your Life "Beloved". When you learn to utilize the tools innately in you to heal and reframe your life, the pain from past hurts begin to fade and the vigilant words that have been robbing you from truly living will begin to become a distant memory.

Many people answer that the most important person in their life is their child, their parent, their spouse or some other loved one. While they may be very important and you would do anything for them, the real answer is YOU! You should be the most important person in your life. Most were raised to believe that putting yourself first is selfish, but the reality is that when you take care of yourself, you have even more to give to others. That's why airlines say in their safety videos, in case of an emergency, please put the oxygen masks around yourself first, before trying to assist anyone else including your child and loved ones.

It's worth considering the health consequences of failing to make your needs your first priority. When someone says, "I don't have time to take care of me like I should", what does that really mean? It means they don't think their basic needs such as sleep, exercise, eating well, taking time to enjoy themselves and relaxation are necessary for them. It means they don't value themselves or think that they are as important as the people nor the things that they are responsible for. The truth is that when you don't take care of yourself, every part of your body, everything else in your life and everyone that's close to you feels the effect. Never sacrifice your own well-being and happiness for someone else. You have loved ones that you should consider to be the most important people in your life, whether it be kids, a parent, sibling, friend or spouse. However, at the end of the day, who really is going to make you the most important person?

I have lived my whole life depending on other people for happiness. I've held on to toxic people just because they occasionally made me feel good about myself. Then one day I realized that I didn't need another person to make me feel good about me, I learned to love myself without seeking reassurance and validation from others. I hope that when you read this, you too, can start to depend less on others and more from yourself because you truly deserve it.

Everyone is worthy of happiness. You should never have to rely on someone else to put a smile on your face. That smile should already be there. When you wake up in the morning, you should look in the mirror and smile because you woke up and today is going to be amazing regardless of what's going on around you because happiness is a mindset, more so than a fickle emotion. It's all about your state of mind. I'm not saying things don't get tough because for sure they do. Everyone has their demons and everyone has their struggles. Maybe you're going through a divorce, a break up, lost job or struggling with a physical or mental illness for which you just can't find the right treatment. Maybe you think you don't like what you see in the mirror everyday. Maybe you battle some sort of addiction. Nevertheless, when it comes down to it, the most important thing is your state of mind and mentality. If you can manage to learn how to turn a negative situation into a positive one, that is when you'll start to see yourself as the most important person.

For me, everyday is different. Sometimes I wake up and I am prepared for the day and I feel great. Other days I can feel like I don't have time for that, whatever "that" is for the day. I have learned to pay close attention to how I feel and recognize when I'm feeling good or not so good. I know that on the not so good days I need to not take things personally or let my lack of patience get the best of me as I interact with others. Pay attention to the types of emotions you go through and notice the little things that could be triggering those feelings for you.

That means you need, and deserve, to treat yourself with the same thoughtfulness, dedication and time that you commit to taking care of everyone else. You do this not for selfish reasons but because it actually makes you a better parent, better partner, more effective employee and leader for your family. You should take care of yourself because you are the most important person to those you love and they need you to be at your best, whether they realize it or appreciate it, it doesn't matter. They still need you to be The ULTIMATE YOU.

Of course, I know the simplicity of this message does not make it easy to do. There are so many ways to begin. I suggest sitting down and answering a few of these questions:

- What do I need right now in my life?
- What is missing from my life?
- What do I wish I could be doing, that I haven't?
- What has been robbing me from my happiness?
- What do I wish I could stop doing now?
- How can I create a little more margin in my life?
- What was my favorite thing to do when I was a child?
- What makes me feel truly relaxed and at peace and how can I do more of it?
- Where in my schedule can I fit in 15 minutes a day, just for me?
- Is there a friend that I have been really missing that I have been too busy to reach out to?
- What can I say "no" to in order to say "yes" to myself?

You don't have to know the answers to all these questions. Just start by asking them to see what it could look like if you took care of you first and treated yourself as an M.V.P.

MASTERING THE ART OF LETTING GO

WE'VE ALL BEEN HURT. You can't be an adult today if you haven't experienced some kind of emotional heartache and pain. It hurts. I get that, but what you do with that hurt is probably more important than the hurt itself. Would you prefer to get back to feeling alive, full of vitality and actually loving life or to continue to be complacent and watching life just pass you by? Maybe you are like some people I know and prefer to sit in a perpetual cycle of hurt and wear the victim mentality, like a badge of honor. Holding on to pain doesn't fix anything for you. Replaying the past over and over again doesn't change it. Wishing things were different doesn't make it so. In some cases, especially when it comes to the past, all you can do is accept whatever it is you're holding on to and then just let it go. Like poof, be gone.

So, how do you let go of past hurts and finally move on? Let's explore this a bit. If you've ever lived in an area in which dandelions grow, it's likely that you've blown the dried seeds of the dandelion flower at some point. Once dandelions turn from their vibrant yellow color to their white/gray seeds, they can be blown, sending the seeds into the air like tiny particles. Sometimes adults hold on to that hurt and that pain of a dandelion in your hands and you refuse to let go of something that is dead. You are not going to forget what they did to you. You are not going to forget those hurtful words said to you. While I understand the logic of not wanting to forget, as a way of protecting yourself to make sure it doesn't happen again, this is not healthy.

Sometimes the solution is just as simple as blowing hurt and pain away and letting them go from you, so you can start living life again. Instead of dwelling in the past you can then begin to live in the present. That's how everything can change for you in this area. You have to let go of what has been hurting you, even if it feels impossible to do so. Deciding to hold on to the past will hold you back from creating a strong sense of self, a self that isn't defined by your past, but rather by who you want to be in the future.

Oddly enough, painful feelings can be comfortable to some, especially if that is all you know. Some people have trouble letting go of their pain or other unpleasant emotions about their past because they think those feelings are part of their identity. In some ways, they may not know who they are without this pain. This makes it near impossible for them to let go. By human nature you become very attached to what you know and believe to be true and this often leads to resistance when offered a real change. Many people have to be pushed or dragged out of their comfort zone, which is actually a place of pain, because they have become so used to it, they've lost sight of how great things could be. Do you know somoene like that? Is that person you?

I have to also talk about those who love to play and live in that victim role mentality. Listen, blaming others for your hurt is what most people start off doing. Somebody did something wrong or they wronged you in some way that really mattered. You want them to apologize. You want them to acknowledge what they did to you was wrong.

The problem with blaming others is that it can often leave you powerless. For example, you confront the person (your boss, your spouse, your parent, your child), and they totally disregard and minimize your feelings, then you're left with all this anger and hurt and no resolution. I remember confronting people in my life, actual loved ones and letting them know how their actions had affected me over the years and into my adulthood. When I confronted them and blamed them for my pain and frustration, the first thing I got was denial everytime. "I didn't do that. I don't even remember what you are talking about. I know I would never say that! I would never do that to you. You have confused the situation and taken this personal when it is not."

While all of my feelings were legitimate, it's important to feel them, process them fully and then move on from them. When you harbor those negative feelings you are doing nothing but hurting yourself further, while the other person has moved on and this situation, this pain and hurt that you are feeling is not even a blip on their radar.

Here's another reality check. The only way you can accept new happiness into your life is by making space for it. If your heart is filled full with pain and hurt, how can you be open to anything new such as happiness, love and support? The answer is, you can't. So remember, if you crowd your brain, and life, with hurt feelings, there's very little room for anything positive. Now you know the adage, "hurt people, hurt people", well it's certainly true. It's a choice you're making to continue to feel the hurt, rather than finally welcoming joy and peace into your life.

Why do you hold on to the past? Why do you hold on to things that are no longer relevant in your life? Why is it so difficult to let go of experiences that have caused you pain and suffering for so long? Think back to the tragic day of 9/11. Chances are you can probably picture who you were with and what you were doing when you heard about the terrorist attack. Now, think back to August 11, 2001, your memory of this day, just a month before is likely not even exisitent. I'm sure only a few people can remember what was happening a month before the attacks. This is because we do not retain information that does not have an emotion attached to it. Information with emotion makes an indelible impression on your mind. A person will attach emotion to anything that impacts them in a significant way, especially if it causes them pain, suffering or sadness. I love music, especially hip hop and R&B. I remember exactly where I was when I found out 2-Pac was murdered. I remember exactly where I was when I found out Aaliyah was killed in a tragic plane crash. Even more recently we all probably remember where you were when we found out about the helicopter accident killing Kobe, Gianna Bryant and seven others.

These events had emotions attached for me, so I will never forget those days.

While these are experiences that have indirectly affected you in most cases, you have experienced pain at some point in your life that has affected you intimately. When this happens it affects your overall well-being and can hurt you, mentally, physically and spiritually. I know, as well as anyone, that pain is a really tough part of life, but how are you supposed to get rid of that feeling is really what you need to begin to ask yourself.

If you are like I once was, you are probably looking for a quick way to get rid of feelings of hurt and anxiety to improve your immediate happiness. That's why many people rely on short term pleasures like drugs, alcohol, smoking, sex, work, exercise and just about anything that will get them a quick fix. The easiest way to get rid of this pain is to learn how to let go of the past, especially the pain that specific people or circumstances have caused you throughout your life. Now, I know what you are thinking, this is easier said than done.

Yes, it is, but you really have no choice if you are going to be The ULTIMATE YOU. Letting go of the past will allow you to live a happier life that is free from negativity. It will allow you to be content with living in the here and now. The transformation that takes place in a person who is willing to let go and grow, is amazing to see. The stages of change usually occur as follows:

IN DENIAL: I do not have a problem.

So let's take drinking too much alcohol as an example. An individual knows the downside of this habit: spends too much money, feels awful the next day, alters their thinking and behavior and often affects their relationships, it's bad for their liver, kidneys etc.

CONTEMPLATION: Maybe I do have a problem.

At this stage the person is contemplating on the idea that this habit is damaging to themselves and others, and is more open to the idea of changing their behavior, however, the addiction is too powerful for them to stop for the long-term.

PREPARATION: I accept that I do have a problem.

This is a huge step forward and usually happens when the pain is too great to stay within the current circumstances. Once the person acknowledges that they need help, they will be more open to allowing others to support them and may actively seek the assistance they need.

ACTION: I am ready to take the steps to rid this problem once and for all.

This is where the rubber meets the road. In the other steps, the person was unable or unwilling to make lasting change, because the short-term pay-off for this vice is greater to them than the long-term transformation. It's usually when someone reaches the bottom of the barrel and they have no where to go but up. They see that their behavior and habits have gotten them to where they are today and they no longer want to stay there and are finally willing to do the necessary and hard work to get their life moving in the right direction.

I know it's incredibly hard to let go of your pain from the past, especially if it has caused a lot of emotional and physical pain for you. I've struggled with this myself. I have held onto things for such a long time, it begins to feel like an old friend of mine. It would give me justification for my feelings and emotions. It would have been sacrilegious for me to let it go, but I had to move on and grow.

Nobody's life should be defined by their pain. It's not healthy, it adds to your stress, it hurts your ability to focus at work and it impacts every other relationship you have, even the ones not directly associated with the pain. Every day you choose to hold on to hurt and pain is another day everybody around you has to live with that decision too and feel its consequences.

So do everybody, and yourself, a big favor, let go of the pain you have been holding onto. Do something different today and welcome happiness back into your life by becoming The ULTIMATE YOU and to start to "Live Your Legacy".

MANIFESTING YOUR DREAMS

IN THE BEGINNING WAS the Word, and the Word was with God, and the Word was God. We could all learn something from this well-known Bible verse whether you are religious or not. Looking beyond the religious overtones, there is a message to be found in this for everyone. Everything begins with a word. For the technical aspect of what I'm about to say, words consist of vibrations and sounds. It is these vibrations that create the very reality that surrounds us. Words are the creator, the creator of our universe, our lives and our reality. Without words, a thought can never become a reality. This is something that has been taught throughout history, as far back as the Bible, which writes of God saying '"let there be light" and as a result there was the creation of light.

What you can learn from this is if words and thoughts are the very tools with which you create your reality, then surely they are your most powerful tools yet. It means you should only pick the very best words in order to create your very best reality.

Your thoughts also impact what you manifest in your life, but it can be argued that the real power lies in your words. It is your words that provide a bold affirmation and declaration of your innermost thoughts. They are a confirmation to the world of how you see others, your life and yourself. It is this powerful affirmation that your words provide which enables your thoughts to manifest into your new reality. So why would you choose to misuse your most powerful asset.

As a society as a whole, we have become conditioned to talk about our misfortunes and problems. We take our interpretations of events, people, ourselves and communicate them to the world, bringing them into existence. By that admission, when you complain about your life to others, you are putting those negative words out there to become your reality. When you say something out loud enough times your words become your truth, not only in your mind but in the minds of everyone to whom you are speaking.

With this being the case, ask yourself, do you really want to tell yourself and everybody that you know that you are unlucky when it comes to love, not being successful, feeling miserable, bored or whatever else you have been complaining about? Especially now that you know that it is those exact words that are creating the life that actually affects the way you live. In the black church they have this old saying, when someone asks how you are doing and one of the older member would say, "blessed and highly favored". I would be like oh, okay then, but while I viewed this sarcastically, this is what you must do. Speak positivity and optimism into yourself and into your reality.

Begin to choose words wisely that you speak consciously. Practice improved self-awareness over the words that you use to describe yourself and your life. Negative, powerless words such as "I can't" should be avoided at all costs. They will strip you of your ability to manifest the life that you want to live.

As the creator of your universe, what you say, goes. Therefore, next time you catch yourself about to use negative words, regain control, reframe your thoughts and adjust your words so that they have a much more positive impact on your world.

For example, if you would usually say something such as "I feel fat or out of shape" then why not turn this into a more positive, constructive statement such as, "I am one day closer to my ideal body". See the difference. One is of negative perception and the other is of encouragement and optimism. Your words are the paint with which you use to paint your reality. Choose these words wisely and positively to create a reality that is good for you and not limiting.

Affirm who you are, your dreams, your hopes and your successes with two of the most powerful words that a person can ever utter, "I am". These two small but incredibly powerful words should be considered the most precious words that you have in your entire vocabulary. How you end the sentence "I am" defines who you are to yourself and to everybody around you. So, when you say "I am fat, lazy or shy" try something like "I am good looking, confident, successful or happy". This will be the exact truth that you are creating for yourself. It doesn't even matter if you don't believe what you are saying in the moment, but how you finish those two little words is how your reality is defined and created.

Why not choose a higher level of expression for yourself? Remind yourself of who and what you are by starting each morning with a positive affirmation beginning with these magical words "I am".

If you have ever seen the movie Malcolm X with Denzel Washington, there was a point in the movie where the film goes through a flurry of clips of many different people saying "I am Malcolm X". This is pivotal, because the people who were saying it were from a society stand point in that day were looked as less than and looked down upon. Malcolm did not stand for this. He wanted and did rise above all the oppression, segregation, hatred and viewed himself differently. So when they say "I'm Malcolm X" they are saying I'm more than what you see me as. I'm somebody. I'm worthy. I'm valuable. I'm lovable.

When you complain about your lot in life, speak anxiously or use hateful words, you usually do so from a place of fear. The first step that you need to take in order to conquer this is to practice better self-awareness over the words that you are using. The next time you open your mouth to complain about something or to put yourself or others down, ask yourself some questions. Why am I about to say this? Is it true? Am I building up or destroying with my words? How is this going to serve me, my happiness and my self-esteem?

If you ask yourself these important questions you will no doubt discover that you are in fact speaking out of a place of fear. This is the fear that you are not good enough, fear that you are in the wrong relationship, the wrong career, etc. Most importantly, you will realize that by voicing these fears you will be doing nothing for your happiness. Your words used this way will only make you feel worse, thus manifesting these fears into your life with greater intensity and you don't want that.

So, choose your words bravely, consciously and lovingly. Always speak from a place of love, for yourself, for your life and for others. Your words have incredible power that can either build, they can destroy or they can be left unspoken.

You have a responsibility to the people you care about. Your words, your validation, your affirmation can change people's lives. This is just as true for your children and your spouse, as it is everyone in your life.

Everyone walks around with a big sign around their neck that says, I need love. Make me feel important. Make me feel significant. Even the guy that flicks you the bird while in traffic when he's upset. What he is really saying is, "you cut me off", "you made me feel unimportant," and "I need love." Think about the person that does an armed robbery. His whole life may have been viewed by others and himself as being insignificant. What happens the first time he pulls a gun out on someone? He instantly becomes very significant! This gives him a high of sorts and at times it may not even be about the robbery, but about that moment of complete significance and importance from others. Not sure if your mind is blown thinking about that, but if we really want to do more to prevent crimes, let's start by making all kids feel loved, valued and significant, as well as, making sure their basic needs are met. Let's give all kids a fair shot at life so they don't end up in a correctional facility, yet again reaffirming their believed insignificance.

This happens in the workplace as well as the streets, but it's more about value than significance. Feeling valued is just as important as how much money you make at work. The need for significance in your work is a manifestation of your inborn hunger for meaning and purpose in your life.

Try this in every room you enter, for every conversation you engage in and interaction you have. Catch people doing something right. Tell them they look good, did something well and that you appreciate their contributions.

Tell your son or daughter today, "Hey, I am proud of you. You are special to me."

In the Law of Attraction, we are taught that you must shift to a more positive way of thinking. The Law of Attraction is not a magic wand, because the brain preferentially scans and stores negative experiences. You have to consciously and habitually build the positive mental muscle in your brain. You have layers and layers of stories, limiting beliefs, fears and blocks that have become the interior landscape of your mind and cannot be changed overnight just by thinking positive thoughts.

In order to become a master at manifesting with the Law of Attraction, you have to undo the patterns that have been stored in your unconscious and replace them with positive, empowering patterns. In other words, you have to rewire your brain.

The Law of Attraction or "The Secret" is the most powerful law in the universe. Just like gravity, it is always in effect, always in motion. It is working in your life at this very moment. You are always in a state of creation. You are creating your reality in every moment of every day. You are creating your future with every single thought, either consciously or subconsciously. You can't take a break from it and decide not to create because creation never stops. Understanding just how the Law of Attraction works is a fundamental key to your success. If you want to change your life, and empower yourself to create an amazing future, then you need to understand your role in the Law of Attraction. You should grow to expect miracles. The Law of Attraction allows for infinite possibilities, infinite abundance and infinite joy. It knows no order of difficulty and it can change your life in every way.

Simply put, the Law of Attraction says that you will attract into your life whatever your focus is on. Whatever you give your energy and attention to will come back to you like a boomerang. So, if you stay focused on the good and positive things in your life, you will automatically attract more good and positive things back to you. If you are focused upon lack and negativity, then that is what will be attracted to your life. Like attracts like as if they were supernatural magnets. If you are feeling excited, enthusiastic, passionate, happy, joyful, appreciative or abundant, then you are sending out positive energy. On the other hand, if you are feeling bored, anxious, stressed out, angry, resentful or sad, you are sending out negative energy. The universe, like a magnet, will respond enthusiastically to both of these vibrations. It doesn't decide which one is better for you, it just responds to whatever energy you are creating and it gives you more of the same. You get back exactly what you put out.

So once you really understand the Law of Attraction, and how it works, you can begin to consciously and intentionally create a better life for yourself. You can choose to respond differently to the situations that arise during your day. You can choose to think differently. You can choose to focus and think about the things you want more of in your life. You can choose to experience more of the things that make you feel good. The Law of Attraction states that you'll attract into your life whatever you give your energy, focus and attention to, wanted or unwanted. You must become more deliberate about what you think and feel. To become more intentional about the thoughts you offer the universe you'll need to decide what you want to experience and really embrace those emotions as you go throughout your life.

Perhaps you want to change your career, move to another state, win a major professional award, become an actor/actress, get a deal on Shark Tank or recover from a major illness. The more you focus on and talk about what you do want (instead of what you don't want), the faster you will manifest your dreams and goals.

After you ask for what you want, you have to believe that you'll get what you want, then take the necessary action just as we discussed with the "IT" Methodology in Chapter 3. I know this is not always easy. Many people have limiting beliefs about themselves, which keep them from allowing abundance and happiness into their lives. If this describes you, realize that you must first change your limiting beliefs into thoughts of you being deserving, worthy, lovable, desirable and capable, as well as smart enough, strong enough, attractive enough, rich enough, good enough and flat out "enough" in every way, shape and form that matters to you. Once you believe that, you'll have no choice to get what you want. The second part of the equation is to take action. Taking action creates your desired results and affirms your belief that what you want is within reach.

As with everything, this all takes time and practice. However, the more you put a conscious effort into attracting what you want and following these steps, the easier it will become. You can begin to expect miracles to happen in your life. For example, if you want to create financial abundance then start by focusing on prosperity and money flowing into you. Envision direct deposits hitting your account. Write yourself a check for the sum of money you wish to manifest this year or take a screenshot of your bank account with your desired balance photoshopped in. Post it in a visible location for you to see daily. Every time you see it, believe that achieving this is not only possible, but a forgone conclusion. Remember to take a moment to be thankful for everything that you already have. By doing this, you are creating a vibrational match for the financial abundance that you want to attract into your future life.

If you want to create an abundance of love in your life, then focus on love. Be the love you want to attract. Become more loving and generous with others and with yourself. By creating the vibration of love, you will automatically draw more of it to you. Focus on whatever it is that you want to create more of and remember to be grateful for that which you already have. Gratitude itself is a form of abundance. The vibrational frequency of gratitude and appreciation will automatically attract even more things to be grateful for, like a domino effect.

Now that you are aware of the role you play in creating the life you desire, you can no longer create your future accidentally or by default. Take this to heart, because this is your moment, your time to begin consciously, intentionally and deliberately participating in the creation of the future you desire.

Your thoughts are very powerful. They are real, they are measurable and they are energy. Every single thought you have is a statement of your desires to the universe. Today's thoughts you think, feelings you feel, and actions you take will determine your experiences tomorrow. So it is imperative that you learn to think and behave in a positive way that is in alignment with what you ultimately want to be, do and experience in life. You don't need to know every single step that it will take to achieve your goals. Just decide what you want. Know that you deserve it. Believe you can have it, then release it and let it go. Open yourself up to infinite possibilities.

Affirmations simply affirm your positive beliefs about yourself and about life. Every thought you think and every word you say is an affirmation. Your thoughts and words are declarations of who you think you are and how you perceive the world to be. Strong, positive affirmations are powerful means of self-transformation and they are a key element in the creation of the life that you desire. They work by purposely replacing the limiting ideas, negative beliefs and negative self-talk that you have taken on and internalized over the years with positive statements that assert who you want to be and how you want to experience life now.

There are no limits on your dreams and goals. The whole world is out there just waiting for you. This is an inspirational technique that you might want to try as well. A great process for clarifying some of your more long-term life goals and dreams is to make a list of 101 goals that you would like to accomplish before you die. 101 things you would like to do, be, have or experience. You could also have a daily vision board that will keep your mind focused on your goals.

Whatever you decide to do, start by opening your mind. Strive to become more aware of the amazing synchronicity that already exists in your life. Remove any lingering negative thoughts or emotions. Remove any doubt and then take actions each and every day that will move you toward your purpose and the fulfillment of your dreams. The Law of Attraction allows for infinite possibilities, infinite abundance and infinite joy. It knows no order of difficulty and it can change your life in every way if you let it. Are you willing to try it to become The ULTIMATE YOU?

THE STORIES WE TELL OURSELVES

DID YOU KNOW THAT we all subconsciously make up stories about ourselves that are not even true. Sounds outrageous, right? Even though you may feel that you don't do this, I hope you hear me because this is vital for you to understand to have an extraordinary life. Have you ever heard of the expression, jumping to conclusions? When facts are missing, your mind starts to fill in the blanks. The problem is when you assume a negative intent is happening when in fact it is not. Where does the brain get this missing information to fill in the blanks? It goes to your past experiences vault and picks a memory whether it has a positive or negative association, it really doesn't have a preference.

The problem with reacting to negative thoughts and stories is it isolates you and keeps good people at a distance when you are incorrect about your assumption. When you assume the worst in people, you lose your trust in yourself and others who may actually have good intentions. Slow your roll and assess the truth of what is going on before moving forward, you will never know the truth if you don't try.

Now telling yourself stories is natural, we do this all the time. There's nothing wrong with it, but if you're not aware of the stories you are telling yourself, they are only stories, not truth nor facts you will not be able to understand how they shape your happiness, relationships, moods and more. Throughout the day, you're telling yourself stories and lies about what's really going on in any certain situation. You have to start to become aware of your stories, both good and bad. Notice them throughout the day. Notice when you're getting stuck in a story, spinning it around and around in your mind. Things like "they shouldn't have done this", making you frustrated and unhappy with that person and you are basing this off of a perceived reality, not a truth.

When you get hooked on a story, it's hard to break away from it, but becoming aware that you are hooked in it is vital to responding accordingly or in many cases not having a response at all. Most of the fundamental stories that you created about your identity was shaped by perceptions from your parents, teachers and significant others. The more consistent the feedback, the more entangling the story becomes with reality as you move through adolescence and into adulthood. So what can you do if you're hooked on a story, even if it's not true? It can be very difficult to break out of that trap. I know, because it happens to me all the time. I see the story I'm telling myself, but it seems so solid and real that I can't just let it go and move on. The first thing I have learned to do is to not act on the story. Even if you're caught up in it, that doesn't mean you have to lash out at someone or run away. Just sit with the story, notice how it's making you feel, notice the physical sensations in your body. Notice that you're caught up, but don't act, just stay with your awareness.

The stories you tell, particularly the ones you're not aware of, can profoundly shape who you are and the decisions that you make throughout life. Recognizing your stories is a hallmark to becoming self-aware and a cornerstone of mindfulness. It can be difficult to void yourself from your stories unless you are conscious of them and understand their origins. Stories end up in a vicious cycle on how you see the world around you. It's like when something negative happens to you, you begin to see the world, those situations, those people all through a

THE STORIES WE TELL OURSELVES

different lens, a filter if you will. For example, if you were sexually abused as a child, you would begin to see sex through a very different lens than someone who was not abused in that way. You would react and act differently around a certain type of person based off this new lens you have. You would avoid or attract the same type of person based on what your lens says. What happens throughout your life, other things will happen negatively. With each incident or encounter a new lens is put on top of the already filtered lens that is over your eyes affecting how you see the world. As you grow up and mature you have more and more experiences affecting how you see the world with those siuations and soon you are no longer seeing anything of reality, but you are only seeing what all these lenses are showing you. Kind of like if you look at life through a kaleidoscope, you are seeing something totally different than what someone else that doesn't have the same lens would see. It's kind of like an alternative universe being seen through your eyes.

What if I told you that life itself is meaningless and we as human beings are meaning-making machines? You hear things, see things, filter them through your experiences, judgements and assumptions to make sense of the world around you and give it meaning. In short, you tell yourself a story. Then you believe it. From your point of view, it is the absolute truth. Given this certainty, you then decide what to do next. You're always making meaning out of things. Always attempting to make sense of the world. It's like putting two and two together and coming up with five, making meanings that are simply not true. Makes you think, doesn't it? There is no inherent meaning to anything. As humans, we invent meaning for everything. When in reality, those life events mean zilch, nada, nothing. It's just something that happened and if it happens again, so what? It happens again. It still means nothing really. You need your meanings to be true to make sense of the world, to make sense of yourself, to put everything in a neatly labeled box. You put yourself in that same box, too, with fixed ideas about your strengths, weaknesses and limitations, all ideas that are artificial and born of trauma. Now is the time for you to let it go because the simple truth about life is that things happen and then other things happen. None of it means anything, even when you force it to mean everything. Life is just a series of events and a transformed life is taking those events at face value and not coloring them with your own judgments and interpretations. A transformed life is joyful and limitless, positive and fearless, honest and authentic. On this side is nothing, on the other side is everything.

For many of you may have so much baggage of hurt and rejection, disapproval and disdain, ridicule and grief, heartache and disappointment that it has been affecting you for years and you probably don't even know it. The thought that you were holding on to this hurt and pain for years and it means nothing. No, that can't be, right? Really. No, say it ain't so! What you need to do is listen to the fact that your relationship with your father, mother, brother, sister or cousin went bad. It doesn't mean they didn't love you. These are the facts, your parents divorced, your dad wasn't around, a family member was on drugs, someone close to you abused you. Those are facts. Then there are the stories you make up about the facts. "Your dad didn't love you. Your mother didn't love you as much as another sibling. Someone else didn't treat you right or respect you. It was your fault that someone violated you." These stories have had you living within a cage of debilitating limiting beliefs born out of emotionally distressing situations where you feel weak, inadequate, worthless or stupid even. That ingrained emotional coding will constantly show up, affecting every area of your life.

The meanings you have created in your head are based on a habit. It's based on some thought that you made up in your mind. Sometimes it's so quick that you don't even see it as a simple thought, an assumption, but you take it as your reality. What you need to learn to do is to be present to your way of thinking, the assumptions and the meanings you make during your day. These meanings and assumptions might be making your life harder. Just keep in mind that everyone is the center of their universe. People are dealing with their stuff and their own thoughts just like you are. So there is good news and bad news. Bad news is, it's not all about you. The good news is, it's not all about you! So, stop tripping in your head. These vicious cycles of stories that have been made up in your head for years have to stop if you are going to live your legacy and become The ULTIMATE YOU.

10

PERSPECTIVE
(OR LIFE AS YOU KNOW IT)

SO YOU ARE HERE because you want to change your life. Well, first thing you need to do is to change your perspective. Everything starts with how you see the world. How you interpret different situations will determine your decisions, actions and reactions. So, if you want to be or achieve something, you have to have the right mindset to get there. You have to get into the right frame of mind so you can be focused, motivated, disciplined, accountable, driven, committed and ultimately successful.

To everything in life, there's always a positive and a negative side. The thing is, it's so easy to focus on one over the other. Many tend to focus too much on the negative things. Watch any local news and you will see the trend there. I have a habit of doing this as well. If one of my sons brings his report card home and he has all A's and one B. I have to remind myself to congratulate him on doing so well in his classes because my first and natural tendency is to be like, son what happened with this B? I totally threw out all his hard work he was able to do with his A's and focus on the one class that he was less than perfect. That's not the type of encouragement he needs, even though I know he is smart enough to get straight A's. See, I have had to learn to shift my perspective.

The good news is that you get to choose which side you want to focus on. It's simply a matter of changing your perspective or in other words, shifting your thoughts. To change this mentality, you need to begin to focus on the lessons of life's circumstances and not on the issues themself. Easier said than done, I know. You go through good and bad experiences throughout your life. You are either in control of them or not. The necessary thing to remember is that every experience is a good experience. The key is finding the silver lining in everything you do. Once you know this, it is fully your responsibility to see and operate in the world with this new perspective.

Now, I'm not saying that all experiences have positive aspects, but it's what you think of that matters the most. There is always an opportunity to grow and evolve.

You should also remind yourself that your energy is like a magnet and it attracts what you put off. You want positivity in your life, you need to give off positive vibes. One way to do this is to express gratitude everyday which will boost your positive attitude in so many different ways. Here's an example of a really easy exercise you should start doing either at night or first thing in the morning. When you wake up, ask yourself, "What are 3 things I am grateful for this morning?" or, when you go to bed, "What are 3 things that made me happy today?" This will help your mind escape any negative things that may have occurred during the day. The more you focus on having a great day when you first wake, the more you will attract it. You will start noticing small details that you hadn't before, like the beautiful plants or flowers that you pass everyday but never really noticed. You will start to see just how beautiful sunrises and sunsets are. On the contrary, negative emotions just make everything seem even more negative and then it just becomes a vicious cycle that sticks you in its sphere of negativity. The important thing to bear in mind here is that your emotions determine your perspective. In other words, if you control your emotions better, you will control the way you see things better. It truly is a win-win situation for everyone involved.

So, as you try to interject more of a positive perspective into your life, you have to distance yourself from the negativity. It's so necessary especially when you start changing your everyday routines and thoughts. Escaping all sources of negativity will give you more space to attract positivity. This also means attracting more positive situations and people. A simple change in how you look at things and events can completely change your life for ever.

Perspective is all about what you decide to focus on. If you decide to focus on negativity, chances are your life is or will be negative. On the contrary, if you choose to realize all the good things going on in your life, the quality of your life will significantly get better every day. It's not about what happens, but how you deal with it, which will determine the outcome.

Remember, it won't happen overnight. If you want it badly enough, like for everything, you will have to take the necessary time and efforts to make this shift happen. If you do this, you will never perceive things the same way you used to. Every day is a new chance and a new opportunity to start again, so embrace it!

11

STOPPING THE INNER CHATTER IN YOUR MIND

WHAT IF WE WERE having a conversation on the phone, over dinner or in a meeting and there was a 90-second gap of absolutely no talking? That's only a minute and a half of complete and utter silence. What would happen? Would you say something just to break the ackward silence? Would you feel obligated to talk or would your inner voice start to chatter inside your head? That inner voice will start to say: "Why is it so quiet? I should probably say something. Maybe I should tell a joke to lighten up the mood. Maybe I should ask a question. I never noticed this feature on that person before. That's a nice outfit she's wearing. Is this dude going to shave down that beard?" Your inner voice will go on and on to fill up that 90 seconds of silence with all types of useless noise. "Did I remember to pack my gym clothes? What do I need to do after work today? I need to call my parents to see how they are doing." This voice is talking to you all of your waking hours and 99% of the time you don't even hear or pay attention to it, but your subconscious hears everything and subsequently you make decisions based off these internal thoughts and conversations.

Wouldn't it be great if you could calm down the nonstop voice in your head? Mental noise is the constant chatter of the mind that never stops. It is the inner conversation or inner monologue that goes on constantly in your mind. It is possible that you are not always aware of this mental noise, because it has become such a deeply embedded habit for you, so much so that it feels natural.

This mental noise is like a white noise machine in a corporate environment. Sounds to be heard, but not noticed. It's the background noise in your mind that never ceases, from the moment you wake up in the morning, to the moment you fall asleep at night. Often, it may even prevent you from falling asleep, as you recall your day, everything that happened and everything that you still have to do the next day because you didn't get to it that day. It is a sort of inner voice that constantly analyzes everything about your life, your circumstances and your relationships. It is a voice in your head that just keeps talking, providing you with different perspectives, good, bad or indifferent. Quite frankly, it is never ending and it never has an idle moment in your head unless you are in a very calm state of mind.

The mind also repeats the same thoughts over and over again, like it is stuck in a loop. Like a S.O.S. signal someone has programmed to play constantly. If these messages in your head are positive thoughts then that's actually very good for you to keep a postive mental state of mind. However, too often, these are negative thoughts that intensify stress, worry, anger and frustration. These are thoughts that you absolutely do not need if you want to have a positive outlook in life.

Thinking is a useful activity required for solving problems, analyzing, comparing, studying, planning and anything else you want to do in life. Too often though, the mind roams and occupies itself with trivial and unimportant matters. Usually it's this useless thinking that wastes your time and energy from the things that should matter most to you. Whether that is your family, your career, your business, your hopes, dreams or your desires. Things like reliving negative past situations or visualizing personal fears over and over again all delay the things that you most desperately want in life. Things like dwelling on the past or fearing the future. These thoughts prevent you from enjoying the present for sure. The past is gone and the future is the by-product of your present thinking and actions. See, the only time that you can control and the only time that exists is right now. This present moment is yours to be seized. "Look, if you had one shot, or one opportunity to seize everything you ever wanted, in one moment would you capture it or just let it slip?" - Eminem

It's that compulsive inner monologue that disturbs your peace and makes your mind unable to rest. You know when you are present somewhere say in a meeting, with family or even driving but you are always thinking about something else, instead of what is going on in the present. If you always have things, ideas and thoughts running through your head, this mental noise often distracts you from everything and everyone that is presently in front of you.

Too often, this inner chatter is tiring and exhausting, and can make you easily sidetracked and unfocused. The mind is a powerful tool, but it also needs to be controlled. Wouldn't it be great if you could achieve a peak state of mind where you can think optimally and be laser-focused when you need to, like solving a problem or making a plan and then after that switch off your mind like a light switch?

Would you watch a movie you disliked multiple times? Of course you wouldn't. So why would you go back in the theater of your mind and revisit thoughts that have caused you pain, stress or trauma knowingly?

Almost every minute of every day your head is full of thoughts, beliefs and expectations that keep your mind racing. You have more conversations with yourself in the course of the day than you do with everyone else you communicate with combined for the week. The truth is, your self-talk is mostly negative and self-limiting unfortunately. In other words, your inner chatter normally limits your potential, impedes achievement and severely damages your authentic self-esteem. If this is the case, there is also a high probability that your communications with others will be the same and for that reason, I will go ahead and say that the quality of your inner chatter determines the quality of your life and your relationships.

Perhaps you believe you are a positive and upbeat person and maybe you are, but the important question is, are you really listening to your inner chatter? How many times a day do you tell yourself that you love yourself, that you're good at what you do and that you are a highly valued member of your family, circle of friends or employer? How many times a day do you applaud your own achievements and praise yourself for even the minor successes? The truth of the matter is, if you are like most people, you are totally unaware of your own inner day-to-day chatter and unconsciously, you will beat yourself up far more often than you will appreciate all that you are.

The best way to remain happy, inspired and confident, even in the wake of some of life's toughest moments, is to consistently be aware of your inner chatter and know you have the ability to manage it. When you allow your inner chatter to run rampant involuntarily, happiness, achievement and a sense of calm is impossible. When you manage your inner conversations and ensure this talk is constructive, positive and loving consistently, this will produce an extraordinary life for you.

So, to become The ULTIMATE YOU you're going to need to become self-aware of your inner chatter and self-talk. Listen to it. How is it talking to you? Would you tolerate a friend talking to you in the same way? Pay close attention to your exact words and write them down. You'll begin to see how the voice in your head contributes to the stress in your life.

Your self-talk, whether you are aware of it or not, either sabotages or supports you. Negative self-talk can result in unnecessary stress, anxiety, depression and self-doubt all brought on by yourself. Positive self-talk encourages self-confidence, effective coping, achievement and a general feeling of well-being. So, ask yourself, is your self-talk building you up or tearing you down? Is your way of thinking helping you or is it hindering you?

THE FORMATION OF YOUR BELIEF SYSTEM

BELIEFS ARE CONDITIONED PERCEPTIONS that are built upon old memories of pain and pleasure. These memories are based on how you have interpreted and emotionalized your experiences over time. It's important to note that beliefs are in deed not facts. However, deeply ingrained beliefs can be mistaken for facts. These beliefs are often nothing more than conclusions you have drawn based on your personal childhood experiences. Back then these misguided beliefs may have served you in a way that was good and protective and that is why you have held onto them for so long. However, as an adult, these beliefs most likely do not serve the same purpose. In fact, these beliefs may actually become a hindrance as they are no longer compatible with your life or your circumstances. Your life has changed, however, your beliefs have remained constant, which is why you're feeling stuck in the present.

Your beliefs are at the core of who you are. They influence every aspect of your life in every conceivable way. For instance, your beliefs will determine your perceptions of reality. They will influence your level of intelligence, impact the decisions you make and limit the choices you even realize are possible for you.

Beliefs also determine how you feel about yourself, how you feel about others and how you feel about the events and circumstances surrounding your life. Understanding how your beliefs influence your feelings is fundamental because they often disguise what's real and instead present you with a false view of reality that only exists in your imagination. As a result, you will tend to make choices based on this false reality with the expectations of getting to your desired outcomes.

Beliefs will likewise determine the things you will or will not do. They will determine what goals you will set and more importantly, they determine how you go about accomplishing them. They also determine whether or not you make the right choices in life from work, to relationships to healthly living.

Your beliefs essentially influence 95 percent of the decisions you make and the corresponding actions required. They form the foundations of how you see yourself in relation to the whole world around you. It's almost as if you have a chip on your shoulder. Have you ever seen someone wearing a "Detriot vs. Everybody" t-shirt, or whatever city is relevant? It's kind of like that. The labels you give yourself, the limitations you put on yourself and the expectations you have of yourself are all built upon your personal belief system. If your belief system is not aligned with the goals and objectives you would like to accomplish, then you will often feel stuck, unfulfilled and sometimes just down right frustrated deep down inside.

So what types of beliefs do you have? For the purpose of you becoming The ULTIMATE YOU, you will want to explore the underlying beliefs that are at the core of your belief systems. These are the only beliefs that matter because they form the foundations of all other beliefs that you hold near and dear to your heart.

Beliefs can be broken down into three very distinct parts: psychological, global and convictions. Psychological beliefs often stem from the pain and pleasure response. The first option brings you pain and the second option provides you with some pleasure or temporary relief.

You will think to yourself. If I do this, what pain will happen? If I do this, then what gratification will come from it? Global beliefs are assumptions you make that begin with "I am...", "Life is...", "People are...", etc. These are total assumptions, biases, prejudices and limiting beliefs about you or a specific group of people. Convictions are the strongest beliefs and are often immune to logic. They are beliefs that have the highest unwavering certainty, commitment, and dedication. Convictions are beliefs that you have built over a lifetime and have a tremendous amount of references supporting them. Each of these references support this belief and builds the foundation for your convictions. Moreover, the amount of emotion, time, energy and thought you have invested in these beliefs over a lifetime makes them virtually indestructible. This is, of course, good news and bad news depending on the types of convictions you hold. If, for instance, you have a set of strong convictions that support your goals and the success you would like to achieve, then you are on the right track. That is in essence how high achievers find the motivation they need to keep going when facing adversity. If, on the other hand, you have a set of convictions that are in conflict with the goals you would like to achieve, then you will likely sabotage yourself and end up making very little progress.

The biggest problem with convictions is that you probably don't even realize you have them. You are so stuck in your own habitual patterns that it's almost impossible to imagine other alternate possibilities. This is definitely an obstacle that you will need to overcome if you truly desire to unlock your full potential.

Beliefs can be things such as how you feel about politics, whether you are on the left or right side. Your natural prejudices and stereotypes about different types of people. Convictions can be things like faith, work-ethic, specific principles you live by, etc.

So now it's time for you to take a step back and look at the belief system that you have created for yourself and the world around you. Take some time to really think about your beliefs, your belief system and where these beliefs came from, whether they are good or bad for you. Make a determination of what beliefs need to stay or go to best serve you in your life today.

PUTTING AN END TO YOUR LIMITING BELIEFS HOLDING YOU BACK

WE ALL HAVE TO learn to challenge the beliefs about ourselves that are keeping us from our greatest potential. You need to train your brain to think differently and you'll open yourself up to brand-new possibilities, releasing yourself from the lies you have believed, even if you have only subconsciously thought about them.

Beliefs are like road signs that point you in the right direction. Without beliefs to guide you, it would be impossible to know how to act, but there's a catch. The right direction is always the one that supports your beliefs, good or bad. Personal beliefs are chronic self-fulfilling prophecies. This is a good thing when your beliefs are positive, as you're likely to create a positive upward momentum that lifts you towards your success. However, you need to learn how to overcome your limiting beliefs because they'll drag you down faster than any crabs in a barrel would.

So what are limiting beliefs and how do they affect your life? A limiting belief is a false belief that you acquired as a result of someone else or you making an incorrect conclusion about you. For example, a person could acquire a limiting belief about their ability to succeed as soon as they may have failed at something. Probably the biggest problem that limiting beliefs cause is that they force you to live below your potential. I remember one of my sons in first grade being so scared to read out loud. At some point he realized his classmates read better than he and another kid must have teased him about reading slower. He then believed that he couldn't read and he refused to read out loud. He took what this other kid said, making fun of him and took this joke on as his truth and it became his perception of reality. He held on to this false statement and he made it a matter of fact for himself. It took about a year of working with him and his reading for him to develop a sense of normalcy and confidence in this area. Even with gaining confidence he still has certain situations when that limiting belief pops right back up for him and he turns into that kid that supposedly couldn't read well. So maybe it's not reading for you. Maybe it's speaking in public, singing, dancing, writing, driving, cooking, playing sports or any of a thousand other things.

Usually a limiting belief isn't just acquired but has been with you since childhood and just stays and lingers with you for much of your life or at least until you decide enough is enough and you work to remove it. Limiting beliefs force people to filter information according to their beliefs. For example, if you believe that you are not a person of worth, then you will only remember those who looked down on you and you will filter out any and all compliments that you receive that say you are important, that you add value and that you are worthy as null and void. After a while, you might not see any value in yourself. What you do not know is that you just fulfilled the prophecy and made your limiting belief become a true and harsh reality for yourself. You brought the thing that you are most afraid of into full fruition for yourself.

Most of the time you're unaware of limiting beliefs. It's like driving with invisible road signs. The signs are there. The directions are there, but you don't or can't see them. If you don't know how to overcome limiting beliefs, you'll find yourself suddenly hitting the brakes when you shouldn't or turning down obscure roads that lead you to nowhere. It's frustrating to spend time and effort trying to get somewhere, only to end up further away from your goal. At the end of the day, limiting beliefs often lead you to lies such as you can't trust people, you are not loveable, you are undeserving, weak-willed, not worthy, incompetent, a failure, not smart, unattractive or you fill in the limiting belief with your own.

So why do we believe these things if they are not true and we know they are false? To the unconscious mind, familiar destinations are the right places to be. People consistently choose the familiar over other options. Sometimes familiar misery is better than foreign happiness. Familiarity is safe, no matter how much it may hurt you.

Deep down, we prefer to stick with the devil we know, rather than venture out and risk encountering the one we don't. What if you could become the person you'd like to be? What if you could get over your thing, whatever that thing is that has been holding you back?

The good news is, this isn't just a hypothetical solution. With some commitment, perseverance and openness, you really can rewrite your limiting beliefs into something positive, progressive and productive.

If you want to know which limiting beliefs you should tackle first, just go straight for the ones that cause you the most pain, heartache or suffering. There are two different ways to overcome your limiting beliefs. The first way is to question them and the second is to forgive yourself for them. These are both really important.

Questioning your limiting beliefs is more of a mental effort and forgiving limiting beliefs works on an emotional level. So, let's work with the previous limiting belief, "I can't trust anyone." You could talk all day about how you might have come up with why you think that and what in your life experience has caused this type of thinking in you. It's very likely you had significant trauma, either physical or emotional and you learned from those painful experiences, "I can't trust anyone." It might have served you at an earlier time in your life, but it's no longer serving you now. In fact, it's probably keeping you from any truly intimate relationship in your life.

So, how do you work with a limiting belief? First thing you need to do is to question it. One of the most basic ways to do that is to see the result of that belief in your life. Say out loud, "Hey, I'm going through life with this belief that I can't trust anyone, but I see that's been hindering me from forming healthy relationships and positive connections and I now see that belief causes me a lot of internal anxiety. It really doesn't feel peaceful. It doesn't feel calm. It's not the way I want to feel." That's one way to begin removing that belief on the mental level. You have to think and say to yourself, this is something I've adopted and it's not working for me any longer.

The second way is to forgive your limiting beliefs by shifting more to the emotional level. You do this by approaching it from a place of compassion and sympathy. If you can't feel that or summon that towards yourself, imagine how you would feel towards a friend that you love unconditionally, a pet or even somebody that you admire tremendously. Center that feeling in your body. Then once you've identified the limiting belief, ask yourself for forgiveness. The script I like to use with my coaching clients goes something like this: "I forgive myself for accepting the limiting belief that _____, and the truth moving forward for me is _____." The first blank is obviously the limiting belief that you've been carrying around. You fill in the second blank with what you feel that voice of unconditional love would say. Channel that feeling or that voice and have that fill in the blank. Example: "I forgive myself for accepting the limiting belief that I can't trust anyone and the truth moving forward for me is that most people in my life really are truly trustworthy and have given me no reason to not trust them and to trust them with minimal guardedness and boundaries". To fill in this second blank you really need to tune in and tap into your heart for your truth.

You can come up with an infinite number of possibilities. If just a baby step is all you feel like you're willing to take, maybe you could say, "The truth going forward for me is that some people somewhere are trustworthy" or "I forgive myself for accepting the limiting belief that I can't trust anyone and the truth moving forward for me is that I'm open to the possibility that some people are trustworthy."

It might sound like a tough question, but just imagine the possibilities. What if you could let go of the thoughts, ideas and limiting beliefs that have been holding you back from your full potential? If you successfully do this, you will open up a world of new possibilities for yourself like you never knew possible.

FREEDOM THROUGH FACING YOUR FEARS

IT IS HUMAN NATURE to avoid things that scare and terrify us. Who wants to walk directly into what promises to be a painful and frightening experience? Most don't, but here's the thing, being scared will keep you hostage to the fear monster for years to come. Typically this involves avoiding any potential stressor or fear. It could be a necessary conversation with a boss or even a spouse. It could be things, like snakes, tight spaces, heights or public speaking. Whatever it is, you can't hide from it forever. It's going to show itself in one form or another, despite your best efforts to suppress it. They say that F.E.A.R. stands for False Evidence Appearing Real and this is true. It's the fear of this perceived reality, experiences and actions that keep you hiding out and living a sheltered life.

An important step in managing anxiety involves facing feared situations, places or objects. It is normal to want to avoid the things you fear. However, avoidance prevents you from learning that the things you fear are not as dangerous as you think.

The process of facing fears is called exposure. Exposure involves gradually and repeatedly going into feared situations until you feel less anxious. Exposure is not dangerous and will not make the fear worse and after a while, your anxiety will naturally lessen.

Starting with situations that are less scary, you work your way up until you are facing things that cause you a great deal of anxiety. Over time, you build up confidence in those situations and may even come to enjoy them. This process often happens naturally. For example, a person who is afraid of the water takes swimming lessons every week and practices putting their feet and legs in the water, then the whole body and, finally, diving underwater. People with a fear of water can learn to love swimming. The same process occurs when people learn to ride a bike, skate or drive a car.

Exposure is one of the most effective ways of overcoming fears. However, it takes some planning and patience. First, what you need to do is make a list of situations, places or objects that you fear. For example, if you are afraid of dogs, the list may include, looking at pictures of dogs, standing across from a dog park, standing in the same room as a dog on a leash, standing a few feet from a dog or even petting a puppy. If you are afraid of social situations, the list may include saying hello to a coworker, asking a stranger a question, making small talk with a cashier or calling a friend on the phone.

When you set up your exposure of the fear that you want to conquer, it's best to use what is called the fear-ladder approach. Once you have made a list of things to do for exposure, arrange them from the least scary to the most scary for you. You can do this by rating how much fear you have for each situation on the list, from 0, no fear, to 10, extreme fear. Once you have rated each situation, you do them from the least to most frightening.

As you are working through these exposure experiences, if the situation is one that you can remain in for a prolonged period of time, such as standing out on a balcony if you are scared of heights. Stay in that situation long enough for your anxiety to lessen or if it is already short in duration, try repeating it, which involves doing the same thing over and over again for a set number of times, until you start to feel less anxious.

If you stay in a situation long enough or continue engaging in a specific activity, your anxiety will start to reduce. This is because anxiety takes a lot of energy and at some point it just runs out of the fuel that has been running your fear. The longer you face something, the more you get use to it and the less anxious you will feel when you face it again.

It is important to plan exposure exercises in advance, that way you feel more in control of the situation. Identify what you are going to do and when you plan to do it. Remember, exposures should be planned, prolonged and repeated!

Once you are able to enter a specific situation on several separate occasions without experiencing much anxiety, you can move up to the next step on the ladder.

The key to conquering your fear is to practice on a regular basis. Some steps can be practiced daily, while other steps can only be done once in a while. However, the more you practice, the faster the fear will fade to oblivion.

Remember, you will experience some anxiety when facing fears, this is normal. It's not easy to face your fears. Reward yourself when you do it. It may be helpful to use specific rewards as a motivation as you begin to conquer your fears. For example, plan to purchase a special gift for yourself, engage in a fun activity, treat yourself to a nice dinner or whatever your fancy. Most of all, remember "you can do it!"

CREATING A LIFE THEME

YOUR LIFE SHOULD HAVE a theme, a motto, a definite thing that you stand for. Does that sound a bit corny to you? It did to me until I realized how much having one could affect all aspects of my life.

I'm not talking about a theme song here, even though I have wished my life had a soundtrack. How dope would that be! Really, I'm talking about a saying that represents the concepts you find most important and vital in your life.

I never thought to look for a theme in my own life until a couple of years ago. I'm a seeker, always looking for meaning. I'm always reading, studying and trying to figure out the best way to do things. With my seeking nature, I'd read often about the importance of finding my purpose in life.

We all have a purpose. Finding the theme that is evident through your life will help you pinpoint exactly your purpose and move you that much closer to connecting it with your passion. Your passion, purpose and life theme are very tightly connected and supportive to one another.

Life themes reflect what you value most and are a major part of your life calling, those things that you are called to learn about, experience and master. Once you know what your theme is you are halfway to understanding what inspires you, what drives you, what motivates you and what gives your life meaning.

Life themes are made up of keywords that represent your highest values. Each value gives you a starting point for defining your major life theme and how it intertwines through the major events and synchronicities of your life. Each represents your personal perspective or viewpoint and thus how you experience the world.

Many people look through the eyes of justice and measure and weigh every experience, consciously or unconsciously, by whether the outcome was just or not. Others value truth and are always looking for it and confused by the lies people tell and the fake news of the world.

Okay, you are probably wondering that's cool, but how do I identify my life theme. It starts by getting you thinking about the one, two or three things that you most value, unconsciously seek out and love to experience. Your life theme is best expressed in your own words, but it is often difficult to figure out how to start.

Clues to your life theme are all around you, if you know where to look and how to see the hidden themes throughout your life. Your favorite things, movies, books, TV shows, etc. are all great places to start. Follow the clues and use them to develop a statement of your life theme, putting the keywords into a short sentence that expresses in your own words why you are here, what you value most, what you are meant to learn, experience or understand by living your life.

Once you have found the right words for your life theme, you will start to see a connection between the way you look at and move through the world and the issues that form the pivotal and extraordinary events of your daily life. These insights will change your perspective, as well as the way you look at the challenges, obstacles and opportunities you face.

A life without a theme seems like an unfulfilled life. The sooner you can determine your theme the better. Think about it, wouldn't it be better to determine a theme early on and then work on it each day? I wish someone would have slapped me into life's reality and told me to develop a theme to my life and then live it with everything I have, because Y.O.L.O.

Developing a theme will aslo give meaning to your life? You already know your life has meaning, but developing your theme will help you define your main idea and supporting narratives to your life's story. It will work to gather all of your life dots and connect them to really make sense of everything. Just like a mediocre story in a book, there may be a residual theme present, but you forget it as soon as you loose your focus and another priority takes over. You don't want to live a mediocre life. Developing your life theme is important to ensure your life is an amazing and well-lived one.

Finding your life theme is as simple as looking for unifying messages in your daily life. In case I haven't convinced you yet, here are some reasons to find your theme.

Having a theme gives you a sense of purpose and clarity in everything you do. Being clear about what you stand for will help you find a community of people to resonate and to bond with. It helps you form new friendships and find new partners. Knowing what you stand for will help you decide more quickly whether certain opportunities are really right for you or not. Knowing what you stand for will help you find more purpose in the work that you already do by aligning with your theme and emphasize that part of it in your daily life.

Having a theme gives you a solid foundation to stand on. You feel more confident about who you are and the message you are bringing with you into every situation. Now that you know how important it is to have a theme, take the time to go and identify yours. Write it down and remember it so you can refer back to it daily.

CASTING YOUR VISION

Do you have a set vision for your life? Do you know what you want to accomplish and what you are working towards? It is important to take some time to discover your vision for your life. Your vision is like having a Back 2 The Future DeLorean and traveling into time and seeing your future. It's an image that makes you feel hopeful and excited when you look at it. It's a future reality that you are willing to work and sacrifice for because the rewards will be far greater than the sacrifice.

Your vision is the image of your ideal life. It represents all the things and people who mean the most to you. Your vision is your own. It is what you want to achieve, accomplish and enjoy during your lifetime. It will encompass the legacy you want to leave.

It's not about being successful. It's not about earning awards or recognition. It's not about having a big house and a fancy car. It's not about making a million dollars. It's about creating a legacy for others behind you. It's about making a difference in the world around you. It's about living a life filled with passion, purpose and joy.

I personally believe we are all put here on this earth for a purpose. I believe it's our responsibility to figure out that purpose and pursue it passionately. The first step to find out your purpose is to create a vision and connect that with your dreams.

Your vision may change some as you age and mature. You may find things that were important to you ten years ago are not really that important now. You may find that you have realized some of your dreams already which is great and now you need to create new ones to start working towards. It is always important to re-evaluate your vision, goals and dreams at least once a year. Most of all, it's important to make sure your vision is so powerful that it encourages you, reenergizes you and keeps you motivated.

A vision is meant to inspire and move you. The clearer you are about it, the greater the impact you will have in the world. When you create your life vision, you operate from a place of fearlessness and limitlessness. By choosing to adopt this belief system, everything becomes possible for you. As the Bible says, "Without a vision, people perish." When you live a life of purpose, you are in alignment with your true self, which allows you to tap into a higher power and turn your dreams into a reality.

What is your purpose in life? Why do you do what you do? Clarifying your vision is one of the most powerful ways to bring immediate change to your life. When you live by your vision, everything changes. Without a vision, you'll be stuck with a life of boredom and mediocrity. Hope will dwindle, work will be monotonous and relationships will be shallow. Many people struggle to discover their vision. Don't let that happen to you.

The reason so few people live out their vision is because they don't know where to start. Vision begins with dreaming. Not pie in the sky dreaming for materialistic things. Things do nothing to motivate people to live their lives long term. A real dream is about living for something that's bigger than yourself. It's your life's purpose, your mission, the reason you were created that motivates you. It's a marathon and not a sprint. How are you going to change the world? What kind of legacy will you leave? What impact do you want to make in the lives of others?

Here's a scary reality, when you are not clear on your vision you are living against yourself. You're living in opposition to who you really are and what you're supposed to be doing with your one and only amazing life. The truth is that you are here for a reason. You are created with intention and unique gifts to share with the people around you. Discovering who you are and what you're supposed to be doing is the most important thing you will ever do.

Now, don't get overwhelmed. If you don't discover your complete life purpose through this process, don't sweat it. We live out our vision in phases and if you are only able to see a small part of your vision now, that's perfectly fine. Live that piece with all your heart and more of the vision will come with time.

A vision pulls people forward. It projects a clear path of a possible future. It generates the enthusiasm and energy to strive toward your goals. Visions are about your hopes, dreams and aspirations. They're about making a difference. They tell you the purpose and greater good you are seeking. Visions are about the extraordinary. They are about what makes you distinctive, singular and unequaled. Word pictures, metaphors, examples, stories, symbols and similar communication methods all help make visions come to life and to be more memorable. Visions describe an exciting possibility for your future. They stretch your mind out into the future and ask you to think big. Visions are about developing a shared sense of destiny. As a leader you must be able to show others how they are a part of your bigger vision in order to enlist them in it on how their actions will intersect with the grand vision of things.

A critical ingredient for a strong vision is to know exactly what you are willing to do and not do to achieve it. Both sides of the coin are equally important in determining how successful you will become. Clarity helps you eliminate those things and activities that don't add value to your life. A clear vision for success enables you to draw from within and tap into your internal resources, skills and abilities and by also tapping into others to propel you forward on your journey. Having a vision keeps you focused.

Make a conscious decision to leave the 97% of people who are addicted to mediocrity and step into the top 3% of people who are living life the way they want to live it and are getting incredible results because they are committed to it and focused on it. In case you didn't know, this is how they do it. This is the first step to creating a new, focused and meaningful life. A life where you start to see your visions become reality. You do have what it takes and these incredible gifts are already inside you. You just have to get them out.

Battles are first won or lost in your mind. When you picture yourself as having succeeded, you are one step ahead. See yourself beyond where you are right now. Create a visual portfolio or a vision board where you put images, photos, drawings, videos, quotes, internet print outs and other visual elements, which show the kind of future that you want to have. Look at these images on a daily basis and let them sink deep into your mind. Soak in the details of every aspect of them. Let them quench your dream thirst. Each morning when you wake up, soak them in and likewise do the same thing at night just before you sleep.

Your vision should be at the top of your mind every day. Reflect and concentrate on the mental images as you sleep and over time you should be able to clearly see the image with your eyes closed. Your visual portfolio or vision board can be a hard copy or in digital format. Take a photo of your vision board and you can even print a copy to keep in other places. Make it your computer wallpaper. You can do the same thing for your phone.

There is something powerful about seeing how the end goal looks. It's a magical driving force. Feel it, taste it and immerse yourself into it, then take action to achieve it and bring it to your reality. Visualize and mentally prepare for achieving it. Connect with your vision and let it motivate you throughout your day and your life.

17

JOURNEY TO SELF-DISCOVERY

THIS LESSON BRINGS US to your journey of self-discovery or better stated, your decision to finally find yourself.

I can say with confidence that the moment you truly start down the path of self-discovery, you will never turn back. Many may ask the question, "What is self-discovery?" or "What do you mean you don't know who you are?"

The dictionary defines self-discovery, "becoming aware of one's true potential, character, motives, etc."

Self-discovery means many things. It means finding your purpose in life, it means digging deep into your childhood and revealing the experiences that have shaped you, both the good and the bad ones. It means realizing what your beliefs are and living by them. The effects of self-discovery include happiness, fulfillment, clarity and maybe even enlightenment. The journey, however, is not always an easy road. The journey can be long, rough and rugged. It can include fear, confusion, misunderstanding, doubt and literally revisiting all your choices you have ever made in life. I like to refer to it as spring-cleaning of your mind, your emotions, your surrounding and can include some people in your life. It requires making some tough decisions and sticking to them. My journey so far has seen me cut some people out of my life. I call these people "takers" or "cancers" even. They were takers because I allowed them to be and it wasn't until I realized that many of these relationships were one-sided, that I decided to cut them out. Others are cancers because their lives involve so much drama, ill-will and even jealousy, so they had to go. Besides cutting these people out of my life, I have also had to completely change the course of my life and start to follow my true passion and purpose. I have started to be very intentional about my life and no longer have to try to meet the expectations from others, which is a super hard thing to do. Now I've had several set backs along the way and I will have many more but, I will never give up.

What I know for sure is that this journey of self-discovery is worth taking. I have become calmer, more self-aware and more vulnerable. I have learned to pay more attention to my feelings and to speak with more love and purpose.

What I knew for sure was that I had been very hard on myself for most of my life. I had not been truthful with myself and had unrealistic expectations that had basically set myself up for continous disappointment. Why do we do this to ourselves? Why do we lie to ourselves? More importantly, why do we allow ourselves to get away with it? When someone else lies to me and I find out about it, I don't accept that, but, we lie to ourselves profusely and even cover up our own lies by accepting them as truth to reassure ourselves that everything will be okay.

My message to you is to stop being your own worst enemy. Stop suppressing your emotions and feelings and start accepting them. Allow yourself to feel whatever it is you need to be feeling in that moment. You will find freedom when you feel from within yourself. The universe will give you back the love that you have finally started to give yourself.

So what are the steps to self-discovery? It starts with knowing yourself. Getting clear about what you want in life. Finding your sense of purpose. Learning what defines you. Understanding what makes you happy. If you stop to reflect for a second, you may find yourself not knowing these things and you are not alone. Most of my coaching clients have a general idea but usually can't answer these questions without a level of clarity gained first.

It may also be that while you are happy with some parts of your life, there could be other parts that you do not like as much. Not being happy overall with your life is an indication that you have some unresolved and deep-seeded issues in it.

Up until now, it is very possible that you've not gotten to know yourself very well. You've been busy running on the treadmill of life. A great proportion of your time has been spent working long hours, slaving away in a job and filling your days with back-to-back activities. Your mind is just too preoccupied with other things and other people and to busy to be concerned about yourself.

Unfortunately, not knowing yourself well can result in an unfulfilling existence. When you have no clear idea about who you are, what your core values are, what your personal beliefs and your audacious goals are, you are likely to allow your emotions and decisions to be externally dictated. Instead of making an independent decision for yourself, you adopt the values, beliefs and opinions of your spouse, friends, colleagues or parents, as your own. Thus, you would have no clue about what your personal boundaries are, even if they have been violated. While others can count on you for support, you are not sure that you can count on others, for you.

Did you know that self-discovery is related to the Law of Attraction as well. If you have no clear idea of who you are, you will have no clarity in what you really want out of life. By doing this you're sending mixed signals out to the Universe. Your desires and intentions keep changing from day to day. By virtue of the Law of Attraction, it will be hard to "attract" the outcomes that you want because your intentions are not clear.

For me self-discovery wasn't always possible. It wasn't possible because I had several blocks in my life that were basically crippling me from gaining clarity. Perhaps you have some blocks, too.

Let me ask you this question. Do you fear the process of examining your life under a microscope? There is the fear of discovering that there can be demons in the closet. What terrifies you is that in the process of self-discovery, you can come to the conclusion that you are worthless or that you are not very likeable. Rather than put yourself in pain, you would prefer to stay unaware about these demons and pretend that everything is fine.

From a young age, you are also taught to appear strong, don't cry or display signs of weakness. You were warned the consequences of appearing weak, emotional or needing help: only the strong survive.

By acknowledging who you really are, you may be afraid that others may see this true you and not like what they see. You fear losing their friendships. Hence, you prefer that others do not know about any of your signs of vulnerability or weakness that you may have. It can be hard to admit that you are not all that great, especially if you are holding a leadership position either at work or at home. Your ego is at stake here. You prefer to put on a mask rather than be your true authentic self.

When you avoid the process of self-discovery, you are basically in denial of the real you. You appear to be functioning but in actuallity you are simmering underneath with all these self-sabotaging thoughts and beliefs. You may not realize it but they are probably the reasons why success has eluded you up until this point or why you have never been truly happy.

If that's not it, maybe you have never been taught to love yourself, even as a kid. How can it be possible to love and accept yourself, if you have been handed more criticisms than encouragement throughout your life?

As all humans do, you crave for social acceptance. It would seem far better to adopt traits, ideas and behaviors of others who are popular. It would be easier for you to choose to emulate others for this external validation as you believe that there is nothing worthy within yourself. If this is the case, it means you may have a low sense of self-esteem.

You might have also been taught that it is best to stifle or put a pin in your dreams. At a young age someone might have impressed on you that "It's easier to make a living on an finance degree than on a degree in design". You were taught to choose a career choice based on what would be more financially viable by the marketplace than your own personal likes and natural inclinations. Even while you have an innate talent for art, you came to the conclusion that it is best not to develop it and to follow someone else's advice for you.

As you grow older, you have fewer and fewer dreams for your life. After all, dreams seldom come true, you may say. The dreams you once had as a child... were left to die in your imagination. Maybe it is that there is so much noise and stress in your life, that there is hardly any time for this type of fantasy living nor self-discovery. You lead a busy lifestyle already, with important deadlines to fufill and multiple schedules that need to run like syncronized swimmers. You simply do not have the time to invest in anything that's not resulting in fulfilling your obligations or your family responsibilities. If you have been functioning this way for so long, why rock the boat? This is normal for most people, right? The process of self-discovery is not just about finding negatives about yourself. It is also about finding love and nurturing yourself. If you are bombarded with mindless gossip, unfair comparisons, discouraging remarks and thoughtless comments, your thoughts are filled with this type of mental noise and it will be hard to find the space for positivity.

So, what blocks do you have in your life? Self-discovery is not a one-day or a one-week affair. In fact, it can take months or years of building a relationship with yourself. You have to also note that your inner self is not going to stay constant either. You are evolving and changing all the time. Additionally, as you mature, you gain insights that make up the true and most authentic you. You will become clearer and clearer on the intent that you sent out to the Universe, because this intent is in perfect alignment with the real you. You will not experience any conflict or sabotage as you have full clarity. The energy vibration of your intent is pure, untainted and strong. By the Law of Attraction, you attract the very thing that resonates well within your self. The more you know you, the more empowered you are going to be. A clear, self-understanding results in renewed confidence, centeredness and strength to live your legacy. You go on this journey of self-discovery and you are well on your way to becoming The ULTIMATE YOU!

MANAGING STRESS IN A HEALTHY WAY

STRESS AFFECTS US ALL. You may notice symptoms of stress when disciplining your kids, during busy times at work, when managing your finances or when coping with a challenging relationship. Stress is everywhere and while a little stress is okay and can actually be beneficial, too much stress can wear you down and make you sick, both mentally and physically.

The first step to controlling stress is to know the symptoms of it, but recognizing these symptoms may be harder than you think. Most of us are so used to being stressed, we often don't know we are stressed until we are at a critical breaking point.

Stress is the body's reaction to harmful situations, whether they're real or perceived. When you feel threatened, a chemical reaction occurs in your body that allows you to act in a way to prevent injury. This reaction is known as "fight-or-flight" or the stress response. During the stress response, your heart rate increases, breathing quickens, muscles tighten and blood pressure rises. You've gotten ready to act in a way to protect yourself or someone else. Have you ever heard of stories of people doing seemingly super human things in a crisis, like a man lifting a car to save someone trapped or being able to lift something they normally would not be able to. This is the body responding to the stress felt throughout the body. Another example of your body reacting to stress is the thing that gets you to slam on the breaks to avoid hitting another car or swerving to avoid being in an accident.

Stress means different things to different people. Some people are better able to handle stress than others. In small doses, stress can help you accomplish tasks and prevent you from getting hurt. Your body is designed to handle small doses of stress, but you are not equipped to handle long-term, chronic stress without ill consequences.

Everyone has different stress triggers. Work stress tops the list. According to some surveys, forty percent of U.S. workers admit to experiencing office stress and one-quarter say work is the biggest source of stress in their lives.

Some frequent causes of work stress include:
- Being unhappy in your job
- Having a heavy workload or too much responsibility
- Working long hours
- Having poor management, unclear expectations of your work, or no say in decision-making processes
- Working under dangerous conditions
- Being insecure about your chance for advancement or risk of termination
- Having to speak in front of colleagues
- Facing discrimination or harassment at work, especially if your company isn't supportive

Life stresses can also have a big impact. Examples of life stresses are:
- The death of a loved one
- Divorce

- Loss of a job
- Increase in financial obligations
- Getting married
- Moving to a new home
- Chronic illness or injury
- Emotional problems (depression, anxiety, anger, grief, guilt, low self-esteem)
- Taking care of an elderly or sick family member
- Traumatic event, such as a natural disaster, theft, rape or violence against you or a loved one

According to many researchers the top ten stressful life events for adults that can contribute to illness:

- Death of a spouse
- Divorce
- Marriage separation
- Imprisonment
- Death of a close family member
- Injury or illness
- Marriage
- Job loss
- Marriage reconciliation
- Retirement

Often when people are faced with difficult or stressful situations, they're left wondering how to deal with them. Sometimes the negative emotions from these situations can feel overwhelming and solutions seem elusive. However, the challenging situations you face in life are often the ones that offer you the greatest opportunity for personal growth, even though the question of how to deal with the challenges you face doesn't always have a simple or easy answer. Looking honestly at your situation, experiencing the emotion it brings up and searching within yourself for the answer can bring often surprising positive outcomes.

Each situation is different and may call for a different response, but some basics of how to deal with stressors or challenges can apply to many situations. Here are some ideas on how to deal with stress when facing a particular challenge in your life.

My personal favorite and the one that works best for me is to get moving. Upping your activity level is one tactic you can employ right now to help relieve stress and start to feel better. Regular exercise can lift your mood and serve as a distraction from your worries, allowing you to break out of the cycle of negative thoughts that will feed your stress. Rhythmic exercises such as walking, running, swimming, exercising and dancing are particularly effective, especially if done consistently.

Connecting to others can also serve as a stress reliever. Have you ever explained to someone what's going on in your life and it's like a heavy burden has just been lifted off your shoulders or maybe you realize that you are not the only one in the world dealing with this type of situation? The simple act of talking face-to-face with another human can trigger hormones that reduces stress when you're feeling agitated or insecure. Even just a brief exchange of kind words or a friendly look from another person can help calm and soothe your nervous system. So, spend time with people who can improve your mood and don't let your stress keep you from having a social life. If your relationships are the source of your stress, make it a priority to build stronger and more satisfying connections as life is way too short not to have great relationships.

Another fast way to relieve stress is by engaging one or more of your senses: sight, sound, taste, smell, touch or movement. The key is to find the sensory input that works for you. Does listening to an uplifting song make you feel better? How about smelling ground coffee or your mom's warm apple pie? Maybe petting your dog or cat works quickly to make you feel at peace. Everyone responds to sensory input a little differently, so experiment to find what works best for you.

Sometimes it can be as simple as getting a little rest and relaxation. Listen, you can never completely eliminate stress from your life, but you can control how much it affects you. Relaxation techniques such as yoga, meditation and deep breathing activate the body's relaxation response which brings in a state of restfulness that is the polar opposite of your stress response. When practiced regularly, these activities can reduce your everyday stress levels and boost your feelings of joy and serenity. They will also increase your ability to stay calm and collected under future stress pressures.

Did you know the food you eat can also affect your ability to cope with life's stressors? Eating a diet full of processed and convenience food, refined carbohydrates and sugary snacks can worsen the symptoms of stress. A diet rich in fresh fruits, vegetables, high-quality protein and omega-3 fatty acids, can help you better cope with life's ups and downs.

Feeling tired will increase stress as well by causing you to think irrationally. At the same time, chronic stress can disrupt your sleep. Whether you're having trouble falling asleep or staying asleep at night, there are plenty of ways to improve sleep so you feel less stressed, more productive and emotionally balanced. As a person who has sleeping issues, I typically wake up in the middle of the night and have trouble going back to sleep. On days that I do some physical activity with my body like exercising, riding my bike, doing a lot of house work that keeps me moving, jogging or something like that, I typically get a full and great night of sleep with no interruptions and it makes the next day much more enjoyable, more productive and stress-free.

Recognizing a problem is the first step towards solving it. By beginning to identify and understand the sources of your stress, you've taken the first step to learning how to better manage it. Remember, you want to manage stress not eliminate it, that is the key. Stress is a fact of life that we all have to deal with and that's okay. Stress is coming, but it's up to you to handle and manage it appropriately in the most effective way for you.

RELATIONSHIP RESTORATION

FIXING A RELATIONSHIP WITH a friend or family member is so worth the time, energy and possible uncomfortableness you will experience doing it. As a society, we think it's okay to end relationships too often without addressing the source of the problem and why the relationship went bad in the first place. This causes unresolved relationships in your life that haunt and affect you negatively on an unconscious level. Fixing a relationship is usually worth the time and effort. Communication and expressing yourself are essential to cultivating a great relationship. Relationships are really the foundation of civilization and a true source of happiness and feeling whole.

Getting complete with someone is a choice to no longer avoid that "something" that has been keeping you distant from another either consciously or unconsciously, because you are dealing with feelings. For example, if you had an argument with someone and you get complete with them, then there is no need to rehash it the next time you see them or no need to avoid that person because you are still upset with them.

Sometimes, there is something left to say that has not been said, it maybe you didn't apologize and after you thought you were complete, you realize you want to apologize or you are the one that wants the apology from them. Other times, you may want to tell them one more time how annoying they are. When that comes up, just remember you already resolved that issue and came to peace with whatever the situation was, so there is no reason to rehash it again. Being complete is to have said and done whatever there was left to say or do, to the extent that there's nothing else left. You are complete with the situation or with someone else's action from the situation.

If you ever wonder if you are over something or someone you will know. When you are being complete, you are in complete authenticity and integrity. An easy limit test to know whether or not you're complete is when the topic at hand holds no more interest to you. You have zero emotional reaction or attachment to it. There's nothing left to work out and nothing left to avoid. It's when the issue is put in the past for good and it's as unimportant as yesterday's weather.

To be complete with something, you first need to address what is incomplete within you. Is it the other person? Is it the situation? This is a big distinction as it lets you know if you are holding on to something against that person or that thing. Unless you uncover what is incomplete for you and deal with that internally, you cannot be complete with another person.

When you decide to get complete with someone, there are some very logical things that you need to do. First, you need to take responsibility for what is incomplete. Once you have done that, you have to learn to let it go and give up any discord and resentment. Then you must forgive the other person and maybe even forgive yourself. When you are being responsible for your life and your dreams, you must declare that person or situation that was holding you back as complete. It's definitely a process and too many people just take the short cut and do lip service completion, but are really still holding on to the hurt and pain of the situation.

I want you to think about at least one person you need to get complete with. I also want you to think about what is incomplete for you with this person. Once you have determined this, I want you to call that person. The purpose of the call is for you to let go of that deep-seeded anger and get complete. The format of the call is not for you to rehash everything that may have happened from your perspective, but quite the contrary. It's for you to let go of the hurt, pain and resentment. So, that looks like you taking ownership of your part in the siutation, argument or altercation. You must own your part and apologize for it and really tell why you are sorry. Say something like I'm really sorry because our relationship has suffered because of my actions or even my reactions to the situation. I'm sorry because I miss you being in my life. I'm sorry because you didn't deserve to be talked to or treated like that. When you apologize don't expect one back in return. Actually don't expect anything in return. You are not doing this to get anything back. You are doing it to get complete, so you can move on. This is all for you, not for the benefit of the other, however, it can be a win-win if their heart is open and willing as well to forgive. Don't rehash and project all of your pain and suffering on that person making them feel defensive, guilty or ashamed.

To give you a real life example from my life, I remember when I had to get complete with my dad. My dad and mom divorced when I was very young and having a good healthy relationship with my father was very difficult for me, as I felt he had abandoned me. So growing up and even well until my 30's, I always held this silent and unknowing resentment towards him. It was the subtle resentment that I never rationalized or even thought about, but the one that was always there that just kept our relationship at a surface level, with no substance, depth or truth.

I had to get complete with him and had to make my proverbial completion call. I first apologized and communicated how I always wanted a deeper, more meaningful relationship with him, but how I had kept myself distant. I kept myself distant because I was holding on to things that I believed to be true about how he felt about me that had no merit, no truth and no validity. It was how my young impersonable brain rationalized the situation on why he was not around. My young mind believed I was the reason he left. I was the reason he and my mom got divorced. What was wrong with me? Why didn't he love me? Why didn't he approve of me? Why didn't he think I was worthy of a meaningful relationship with him?

If you have ever seen The Fresh Prince of Bel Air, or reruns of it, there is an epsiode in Season 4 called, "Papa's Got A Brand New Excuse". This is the epsidoe where Will's father suddenly shows back up in his life and abruptly leaves again and Will has an emotional scene with Uncle Phil. Feeling frustrated Will tells Uncle Phil how much he has done and learned without his father and how much more he is going to still continue to do without him. As he says all this, that little boy inside of him that deeply wanted the affection from his father, comes up and emotionally asks Uncle Phil. "Why doesn't he want me, man?" The two embrace. If you have ever seen this episode, it's a very impactful one and one of the best acting scenes in Will Smith's career. This silent pain and rebellious nature was me for a majority of my life. Saying how much it didn't bother me, even though that little boy trapped inside my man body was desperately in need of my father's love, approval and affirmation, but I was too afraid to admit it and too immature to even recognize it.

I tried to get complete with my father on two occassions, years a apart. The first time was not successful. I basically had an emotional vomit on him and told him all the stuff that has happneed that made me feel the way I did and basically putting all the blame on him. I was expecting him to apologize and to fix everything. He, like anyone else would be was taken back, and became very defensive and unable to hear my heart because my communication was flat out terrible.

After about five years had passed, I tried again and I had a totally different experience and outcome. This time I apologized for holding on to those thoughts and feelings for so many years, decades really. I told him that I recognize my feelings, my insecurities and my beliefs have been holding us back from having a true authentic relationship and that I was sorry.

What probably followed was the best, most authentic conversation I have ever had with my father, ever. During this conversation a lot of great things were said but things didn't magically change overnight. I didn't just suddenly lose all those thoughts that were in my brain to new happy thoughts about my new relationship with my dad, no. Overtime what happened was that I slowly began to retrain my brain to think differently about him and about our relationship. It is such a freeing exercise, to get complete with someone.

So, who is it in your life that you need to get complete with and why? This week, I want you to call that person and get complete with them. I mean really don't dwell on who you are going to call and what it may look like to that other person. Don't contemplate on when is the right time to call or what you are going to say. The hardest thing to do in the entire process is to pick up the phone and make the call. So just pick it up and call them. It's kind of like ripping a bandaid off vs. peeling it off slowly. If they don't answer, no worries, you keep calling every day until they do. The point is for you to get complete with them and restore the relationship to its purest and greatest form. This process is more like easing in to a cold pool on an overcast day. Sometimes you can creep in little by little, to let your body adjust to the changing temperature, but sometimes it's best to just jump all in. This is a time that you must jump in!

20

SUCCESS AND YOUR NEW DEFINITION

WE ALL WANT SUCCESS. You want to be and to feel successful. You chase money, fame, power, education, relationships and a thousand other things without ever stopping to ask one essential question. What actually is success for me? Few people pause to consider what it truly means to achieve success in their own lives. As Jim Rohn said, "If you don't design your own life plan, chances are you'll fall into someone else's plan. And guess what they have planned for you? Not much."

If you don't answer this question for yourself, you can end up pursuing someone else's version of success. You can actually make it to the top only to discover you climbed up the wrong mountain. I don't want you to achieve your goals only to realize they were the wrong ones in the first place. It's a disaster few people are able to recover from. In the classic movie Office Space, Michael Gibbons says to his doctor, "So I was sitting in my cubicle today, and I realized, ever since I started working, every single day of my life has been worse than the day before. So that means that every single day that you see me, that's the worst day of my life."

How do you avoid a similar fate? Those who have achieved the greatest amounts of actual success are those who are crystal clear on what it means to reach the top of their game. If you want to follow in their steps, you must achieve equal clarity.

Before you can pursue success, you need to understand what success isn't. If you spend just a few minutes on social media, you'll realize how many people hold a very narrow definition of success. They think it's about building wealth, having the perfect relationship, having the perfect body, launching a million-dollar business or amassing a large social media following. Many times, you probably attach famous people to your image of success.

None of these things or people are wrong, but being like them doesn't necessarily make you successful. Many people have fought and struggled to the top only to feel miserable and burned out once they got there. They're unhappy because they pursued the wrong definition of success. They achieved one that didn't match their values.

Throughout childhood and early adulthood, you learn various ideas of success from your parents, teachers and friends. Everyone has their own agenda and idea of who you should be. Although it's OK to value the opinions and hopes of others, you shouldn't necessarily adopt them as your own. No one can impose their vision of success on you. No one can tell you what it means to live a successful life for you but you.

It's easy to assume that success means obtaining a specific object, such as a specific job title or social status. That if you get that thing or reach that point in your career, you'll be successful. Sometimes the greatest successes are a result from the worst failures. Winston Churchill said, "Success is not final, failure is not fatal. It is the courage to continue that counts."

Don't believe me, well check this out. Before becoming a U.S. president, Abraham Lincoln was defeated for the State Legislature, had failed in business, was defeated for Speaker of the House, was defeated for Congress, was defeated for the U.S. Senate, was defeated for nomination as vice president and was defeated again for the U.S. Senate. If you rest your definition of success on one or two achievements, there's a good chance you'll be very disappointed. In an even more practical and recent example, Lebron James has been to the NBA finals 10 times and only been able to take home the elusive Larry O'Brien Championship Trophy four times. Does that fit your definition of success? How about Michael Jordan who through 15 years in the NBA, made it to the finals 6 times and won 6 times. Is that success?

You must set your goals, objectives and trajectories based on what you desire, not on what someone else wants for you. Some people find that helping people brings them the most joy. Therefore success for them looks like a life giving to others. Some believe that building their business will bring them happiness. Some prefer isolation and others prefer constant activity.

The simple, yet profound, truth is that what makes me happy doesn't make you happy and vice versa. My vision of success probably looks nothing like yours and that's how it should be.

If you fail to define success for yourself and try to pursue someone else's path, you'll end up frustrated, unhappy and ultimately feeling unsuccessful deep down inside, no matter what or how much you end up accomplishing. Bruce Lee said, "Always be yourself, express yourself, have faith in yourself; do not go out and look for a successful personality and duplicate it."

The path to success begins by asking yourself, what makes you happy. It's also essential to understand that in many ways, you already are successful. If you assume that you are a failure until you reach a specific goal, you will never be happy and you will never be content. You have to recognize all you have already accomplished up to this point and see the success in those things.

Ask yourself the following questions. Where have you already seen success in your life? How can you continue building on that success? What lessons have you learned from those successes? What have you learned about yourself from those areas?

Success is both a goal and a journey. When you reach certain milestones, that is an element of success, but you don't stop there. You have to push higher and harder, striving for more as you strive for greatness.

Tony Robbins says, "The path to success is to take massive, determined action." This is great, but how do you find your path? What steps do you need to take to achieve true success?

You must be able to clearly answer several critical questions. What truly matters to you? What are the things that set you on fire with passion? What do you want to make of your life? What lifestyle do you want to achieve? Who do you want to be? What do you want people to say about you after you die?

The answers to these questions must be ultra-specific. It's not enough to say, what really matters to me is being happy. If you can't answer completely, you won't really know what success is for you or where you should be going. You have to be able to see your vision of success.

Before you can begin moving forward, you must assess where you are now. This is a time for honest evaluation, not rose-colored glasses. Where are you currently successful? Where do you need to grow? What are your weaknesses and strengths? Try bringing in a friend or colleague to act as a real and unbiased sounding board.

After that, it's time to set some specific goals for yourself. These goals should be achievable and concrete, but still challenging. Your goals should also be measurable. Say you want to read more to be more successful, set a goal of 12 books per year, not just the goal to "read more". How about read one book every month. Get an audible subscription so you can multiply your efforts in less time, like listening to 2 audio books per month.

If you don't define your success, someone else will define it for you. Do you have yearly objectives at work that define what success will look like for you. Your personal life should be the same way, but objectives defined by you. "This is what success looks like this year for my finances, my relationships, my health, my career, etc." What mountain are you climbing? Is it the right one or are you going to reach the summit and see your mountain off in the distance? Start on the right path today.

I implore you to put in writing what success is for you and to share it with others. Doing this will give your life meaning. Your success should always derive from the values and principles that you hold very close to you because these will stand the test of time, through good times and bad, while giving you a level of consistent success.

21

LIFE MASTERY

THERE IS POWER IN mastery. How many people do you know who are really committed to life mastery today? Most people dabble in a million things, master nothing and wonder why they're unfulfilled. They may have great wealth but lousy relationships. They may be incredibly fit and healthy but struggle with debt. They may have a career filled with achievements but feel heartbroken and lonely.

An extraordinary life is balanced on all levels. You probably know by now that if your aim is to be happy and fulfilled, then piling up huge amounts of money and material possessions isn't going to do it. Unfortunately, most people still believe that this is the key to their success and happiness in life and, as a result, their beliefs drive their actions and their actions determine their results. I get it, I really do. I felt the same way for a long time, but through a series of critical experiences in my life, I discovered that... yes, money is important, but it is not the only area that requires your focus.

As Jim Carrey said, "I wish everyone could get rich and famous and have everything they ever dreamed of, so they would know that's not the answer." If you really want to live a life filled with joy and fulfillment, you will have to master a few other fundamental areas and that's what this chapter is all about. It will challenge you to look at your life and where you want to go and achieve in a holistic way, because thinking holistically will help you make sure you don't end up winning in one area of life but losing in another. There are eight fundamental areas you need to master to finally become The ULTIMATE YOU.

First, health and fitness is your most important one. You and I both know that all the joy is taken out of life when you are unhealthy. When you are constantly exhausted and fatigued, when you don't even feel like getting out of bed in the morning, when you can't find the energy needed to do the things that matter most. When you feel this way, you are not the only one affected by it. The way you feel affects everyone else around you, too. That's not a good place to be and you know it. You also know that your body is very much like the house you live. The strength of the house depends on the strength of the foundation it is built on. The same is true for your body. If you don't build a strong foundation, you'll soon find yourself with a structure falling out of place. Unfortunately, most people think that "once I achieve X, Y, Z goal, I'll get back in shape." It doesn't work that way. You don't want to be the richest man in the graveyard, because what good is your money if you've lost your health along the way. Look, you already know that maintaining physical fitness will help raise your energy levels, release the toxins in your body and boost your metabolism. It can also facilitate the release of those neurotransmitters, called endorphins.

Your body really is a complex machine and a magnificent mechanism and keeping it streamlined and in shape is fairly simple. Nevertheless, people make it more complicated than it needs to be. The more complex you make it, the less likely you are to execute the things needed to keep it moving optimally. So let me make it very simple for you. At its core, the physical aspect of your life consists of three fundamental activities.

Eating, which includes everything that you already know. Having a balanced diet, hydrating yourself regularly, avoiding excessive alcohol, not eating junk food, eliminating or reducing processed fats, including nuts, fruits and vegetables into your daily diet, etc.

Engage in physical exercise on a regular basis, whether it be walking, doing body-weight exercises, swimming, cycling, running, weight lifting, you name it. Try making it a priority to move and be active at least 30-60 minutes a day, no matter your age.

Sleeping is also key. Missing a few hours of sleep on a consistent basis can have some terrible consequences on your mental and physical performance. Sleep continues to be one of the first things people sacrifice to get other things done. There's enough research to prove that for a good night's sleep, you need between 7 to 9 hours. Getting the right amount of sleep at night can make a profound difference on your brain and your heart. The key here is consistency. Also, consider taking a brief nap, only like 15-20 minutes in the middle of the day, if possible. This will make sure that you stay focused, creative and energized for the entire day.

The bottom line is, knowledge by itself doesn't bring about change. The real question is are you going to do what you know to do? As Edward Stanley once noted, "Those who don't make time for exercise will eventually have to make time for illness." So please don't ignore your health. Take care of your body and be aware of the consequences of doing otherwise.

Second, emotional mastery is another key to becoming The ULTIMATE YOU. I think it's safe to say that your emotions will define the quality of your life. Therefore, if you want to experience life to the fullest, know that this is an absolute essential pillar that requires mastery. One of the most profound studies on this subject was done by the psychologist Daniel Goleman, who popularized the term "Emotional Intelligence." In his book with the same name, he offers five key areas that determine your emotional quotient (EQ).

1. <u>Self-Awareness</u> - To me, this is the iron quality of a successful life. Self-aware people master their emotions instead of letting emotions master them. They follow Socrates' mantra: "Know thyself." They're willing to take an objective look at themselves by exploring their strengths and weaknesses and making necessary changes along the way.

2. <u>Self-Regulation</u> - This refers to the ability to control emotions and impulses. Do you easily get angry? Even worse, do you stay angry for a long period of time? Are you a jealous person? Do you find yourself unable to let go of past resentments and suffering? Well, most of us are like that, but self-regulating people don't allow their emotions to take over their decisions. They learn to control their emotions and they think before they act.

3. <u>Motivation</u> - People with high emotional intelligence know how to motivate themselves. They don't rely on external sources of motivation because their primary drive comes from within. They're disciplined, highly productive people who understand the value of long-term thinking over immediate gratification.

4. <u>Empathy</u> - Empathy is the ability to put yourself in someone else's shoes. It's your ability to understand the wants, needs and perspectives of others. Empathetic people are those who can lend an ear when you most need it. These are the people who have brilliant listening skills. They seek first to understand, then to be understood. They realize that the specific situation does not matter more than the person itself. They understand that what happened to others could've easily happened to them. As a result, they avoid criticizing and judging others, which helps them build genuine and beautiful relationships with those around them.

5. <u>Social Skills</u> - Also referred to as people skills, social skills are another critical component of high Emotional Intelligence. People with great social skills are usually easy to talk to. They're good team players and you'll usually see them in leadership positions. People with good social skills understand the value of a genuine smile, the importance of good posture and they typically have great persuasive skills. They shine at building and managing relationships and they're outstanding communicators.

The third building block for becoming The ULTIMATE YOU is love and relationships. You should nurture your emotional well-being in the relationships you build. You should create a long-lasting, passionate connection with another person. You know that love and connections are among some of your most important needs. You know this because you are a social creature by nature. You are wired to connect with other human beings. That's why the absence of good relationships in your life can make you feel lonely, depressed and anxious which, as a result, leads to low levels of self-esteem and self-confidence, which is not good.

To make sure that you don't fall into this trap, as simple as it may sound, you've got to surround yourself with people you love, people who challenge you and hold you to higher standards, people who help you become the person you are capable of becoming. Surround yourself with friends who will be there for you not only when everything's going great, but more importantly, when everything is falling to pieces. Nurture the relationships with your family and especially with your spouse, children and even your parents. Don't take them for granted. You should be nurturing your most intimate and important relationships. These types of relationships can bring you the most pleasure and satisfaction, but they can also be the biggest source of pain and suffering.

One of the greatest lessons and stories I have heard on finding love is this. A man once asked his father, "Father, how will I ever find the right woman?" His father replied, "Son, don't worry about finding the right woman. Focus on being the right man." I believe this little story says it all and it applies equally to both men and women. On your path to mastering these five elements of Emotional Intelligence, relationships are a great starting point for a foundational pillar.

The fourth building block is your career & business. If you can only learn to work on you as you do on your job, your life will be in such a different and better place. Think about it, you get paid for bringing value to the marketplace. You don't get paid for the time you spend on the job. Many people that don't punch a time clock, have jobs that they get paid primarily for the value they bring to the table. That means you don't need to change your boss, your colleagues, your industry or the economy to get better results at work. All you have to do is to change yourself, because if you will change, everything around you will be forced to change as well.

Therefore, if you want to increase your income, all you have to do is to find ways of increasing your service, thus increasing the value you bring. Remember, the rewards in life will always match the service and value that you can provide.

Another way of putting it is that if you want to have more, you have to become more. You do that by learning new skills and strategies in your primary field of interest. Develop your expertise. Discover ways to become more productive at what you do. Learn how to leverage your strengths and how you can have a bigger impact on other people's lives. Build your character. Work on your attitude. Surround yourself with people who are playing the game at a higher level than you. Work constantly on improving yourself. If you'll do so, you'll never have to worry about money again. This is such a simple concept, but it's a critical one to understand fully.

Fifth, is your money and your personal finances. They say that money is like good health, in that the more concerned you are about it, the less you have of it. Despite that, some people still believe that money is the root of all evil and that it is unimportant. Strangely enough, these are the same people who are almost always broke. Let's make this clear. Money is not bad, and it is vitally important. Think about it. The food you put on the table, the clothes you wear, the bills you pay, the medical care and the education you can afford are all things that require money. Yes, money, by itself, won't bring you happiness, but the things and the experiences it will help provide can. It surely brings more happiness than poverty does, wouldn't you agree? You see, money is just a tool and you're either its master or you are its slave. You've got to decide. For example, a knife can be used to spread some jelly on your bread or it can be used to cut someone's throat. A terrible analogy, but it proves my point. It's the same thing with money. You can either use it for good or for evil. That's why I personally believe that money will only make you more of what you already are.

If you are going to have lots of money you have to be a smart and and good steward of it. If you don't have the knowledge to manage a thousand dollars, you'd better stop praying for a million dollars and start learning what to do with that thousand. The best thing you can do is to start early, when the amounts are small. Remember that it's your thinking and your financial education that solves problems. That's why I always emphasize this point, don't focus on what you have or on what you'll get. Focus on who you are becoming along the way. Don't let money define you. When you decide to make an investment, just remember that investing in yourself will be one of the most profitable investments you can and will ever make.

Sixth, is your productivity and performance. Time is, by far, one of life's most valuable possessions. However, despite popular belief, you can't really manage time. Think about it for a minute, how can you manage something which cannot be controlled? As far as I'm concerned, everyone is given only 24 hours during the day. No more and no less. You can't stop time, you can't get more of it and you can never get it back. What you can do is manage yourself in relation to time. In other words, instead of saying, "I need to manage my time better", what you should really be saying is, "I should manage myself better!" How you manage yourself eventually reflects on your personal productivity, at home and at work. There's a common myth that I don't want you to fall into. Let me explain.

We've grown in a system that praises busyness. In fact, we believe that life is not valuable if it's not loaded with a hectic schedule. We're always trying to do more, and more, and wonder why we find ourselves running through life like we are on a hamster wheel. Have you ever looked up and the year was almost over and you thought to yourself, where did the year go? That's because you have mistaken movement for achievement and a lot of activity with productivity. What you have failed to realize is that productivity is not about being busy all day. It's not about trying to cram more tasks into your daily schedule. Productivity and high performance is about getting the most important things done and making more time for the things and people that matter most in life.

For you, that may mean having the time to hang out with your friends, spending quality time with your family, taking your kids on that camping trip, working on that side-business you've started or going on a relaxing beach vacation.

Whatever it is for you, I'm here to tell you that you can absolutely attain it. You can get meaningful work done. Work that really matters to you. Work that is aligned with your purpose, what you value and what you want most in life. So, as you probably understand by now, learning how to become more productive, energized and focused is perhaps the single, most important skill that you can learn and start to implement in your personal and professional life that will continue to pay you dividends for the rest of your life.

Seventh up is personal growth beause if you're not growing, you're slowly dying. Jim Rohn said that, "Formal education will make you a living. Self-education will make you a fortune." It took me a while to understand this concept but I have finally got it and now have taken it to heart. If you're not growing, you'll never be happy. Period. "Don't wish it was easier, wish it were better. Don't wish for less problems, wish for more skills. Don't wish for less challenge, wish for more wisdom." - Jim Rohn

Last, but not least, on the list of becoming The ULTIMATE YOU is contribution. If you grow, the last thing becomes possible for you and that is to have something to give to others. If you just give to yourself, you will not feel alive. You've got to contribute beyond yourself to feel like your life is meaningful. As Tony Robbins said, "Life is not about me, it's about we". By creating happiness for others, you'll end up creating happiness for yourself in return.

To be happy, you must go above and beyond the call of duty to make others happy. It's really that simple. Giving is a powerful tool to bring good fortune back into your life. Of course, it must be authentic. It must be genuine. It must come from your inner willingness to help, not imposed from an ulterior motive. Also, it has nothing to do with money. Yes, you can give money to the local church, you can give money to charities and you can give money to those in need. These are all forms of giving and contribution. However, financial contribution is not the ultimate form of sacrifice.

The ultimate form of sacrifice is giving of yourself. From going the extra mile on a project, to doing acts of service around the house, from smiling and saying good morning, to leaving little notes of gratitude to the people that matter to you, a compliment to a coworker, a handwritten note of appreciation, inviting someone to get ahead of you in line. These seemingly insignificant little things are wonderful forms of giving wholeheartedly and they'll also contribute to elevated levels of happiness for everyone involved.

Contrary to popular belief, life is not just about seeking pleasure and avoiding pain. Life is really about creating meaning. Meaning does not come from what you get, it comes from what you give. As all the ancient wise ones and spiritual leaders have taught, it's not what you get in life that matters, rather, it's who you become and what legacy you leave behind.

Mastery takes time, persistence and determination. No matter how high or low you've rated yourself in any of your life areas, there's always room for improvement. You truly deserve to live an extraordinary life and it will take excelling in all of your life areas to reach it. You'll have to achieve a level of mastery in your health, in your emotional management, in your relationships and in your career or business. You'll have to master personal finances, take your productivity to the next level and invest in your personal growth. Ultimately, if you truly want to live the life of your dreams, you'll need to consider contributing to a cause bigger than yourself. I wish that for you and I really hope that this will help guide you on your journey to becoming The ULTIMATE YOU!

22

WORK-LIFE BALANCE

For most, juggling the demands of a career and a personal life are an ongoing challenge, especially at a time when many companies have slashed their ranks and expect more from the survivors. Achieving the elusive "work-life balance" can often feel like an impossible goal, especially for people who strive to give everything 100%. In today's "do more with less" competitive reality, how can you manage your career and family while feeling satisfied that you are doing both well?

People who study workplace culture emphasize that someone's best individual work-life balance will vary over time. The right balance for you when you're single will change when you marry or have children. Experts also say that a few small steps can go a long way towards staying sane, managing work and home responsibilities.

First, prioritize. If you want more balance, you have to force yourself to be more selective both personally and professionally. Consider all the things that compete for your time and decide what to keep and what to discard. If you spend time doing too many things outside of work and home, then select the most meaningful one, focus on it and stop scattering your attention everywhere. Focus on the things that are most important and don't do the extraneous unimportant things. It's a discipline that doesn't come naturally to most.

If your job allows you to telecommute, which many figured out is perfectly doable since the global pandemic, consider working from home at least one or two days a week. When discussing this option with your employer, approach it from a position of strength. Describe how the flexibility could ultimately help your company. Consider saying, I like my job, and feel that I'm an asset. I'd like to talk about ways I can make my work here as productive as possible and bring more value to the organization. I'm in a not-so-unique situation of caring for my young children, my elderly parents or whatever your situation may be and working from home once or twice a week would give me much-needed margin in my day and I would be able to give you better work, since I would be less distracted.

You might be surprised to find your employer sympathetic, particularly if you're a top performer and adding value because they may be in a similar situation themselves. In this economy, employers that can't give raises might be willing to offer other benefits. They want to treat their best employees well so that when the economy does turn around those employees don't flee to other companies.

Tech is a good servant, but a bad master. Remember that iPhones and other devices exist to make your life easier, not to rule it. Identify certain times, like dinner, when your household must remain tech-free. Come up with email windows at work. Mention this window to your boss and coworkers. Say something like I only check email 3 times a day or only check email between these hours because the rest of the time I'm being very productive with my high priority projects. You don't have to respond to every email or voicemail in real time. Just because someone else deems something a priority, doesn't mean you have to.

Let's get down to the best way to come up with more work-life balance. The first step to work-life balance is determining the most important long-term goal for each area of your life including work, personal, family, health and spiritual. If this sounds difficult and daunting that's because it is.

Choices overwhelm you in life. There are 20 brands of toothpaste at the store, hundreds of dating profiles on Tinder and a thousand different things you can choose to do with your time on any given day. School teaches you a lot, but they don't teach you how to think about who you are and what you want in life. If you have ever been to Cheesecake Factory you saw that their menu is long and exhaustive. They have every type of food imaginable, which makes it very hard to decide what you want. Same is true about life. Is your life goal to get promoted in your current company or do you want to do something completely different? Do you eventually want to have kids or is getting married enough? These can be important questions you might be afraid to get wrong so you will hold off answering them usually.

Unfortunately, not making a decision can be worse than making the wrong one. When you don't know your goals in life, you wander aimlessly, or worse, you let someone else set those goals for you.

To figure out your goals, you have to ask yourself what's the one thing you want to accomplish in life, that by doing it, everything else would be easier or unnecessary? Apply that question to your career, your personal life, your spiritual life and to every other life area.

It takes a lot of time to answer these questions, so don't rush your answers. Take your time and really sit with these things. You'll know yourself better because you'll know what's important to you versus not.

Give your goals serious thought but keep in mind that they aren't final. You can always change goals as your priorities in life change. It's always better to work towards a goal and adjust along the way than to wander aimlessly and let other people dictate where your life is headed.

Once you have a long-term goal, extrapolate it into many smaller goals. Apply the same methodology to a one-year goal, a one-month goal, a one-week goal. Eventually working your way back to what you should be working on right now. When your goals are aligned you'll always be working toward your long-term vision for your life, even in the short-term.

Certain goals will be more important to you than others. Maybe it's important that you're married before you're 35. Maybe you want to be the CEO of a Fortune 500 company. Maybe you can die happy if you complete your collection of Marvel Action Figures. There are no answers too big or too small.

Think about where your career falls on your priority list. People generally approach work in one of three ways. One way is the job orientation types, meaning work is a means to an end. These people treat work as a way to support their personal goals, family, hobbies, traveling, etc. A second way is the career orientation types that work is a way to earn external validation. These people work to climb the ladder and earn status, achievement and prestige.

The third way is the calling orientation people whose work is their identity. These people view work as integral to who they are and they have the desire to be fulfilled through work.

You should resonate with one of these orientations more than the other. This isn't to say that you don't want elements of the other orientations, even if you see work as a way to support your lifestyle orientation, that doesn't mean you don't want work to be somewhat fulfilling. Just because you want to climb the corporate ladder doesn't mean you don't want to spend time with your family.

Figure out what more work-life balance means for you. Your orientation will influence what your definition of work-life balance means. You can then dig into why you feel unbalanced and then how to actually fix it. For some, work sustains their personal interests. These workaholics try to maximize time pursuing their real interests and minimize their time working. Unfortunately for them, the 40-hour work week is dead. The average work week in the U.S. has climbed to 47 hours. Half of salaried full-time employees work more than 50 hours each week, unlike 20 years ago. Work doesn't stop when you leave the office. Work is always just one phone call, email, text or notification away. This is why you get frustrated when work cuts into your personal time, when you have to check emails on vacation or miss dinner because of a late night working.

So if this is you, what do you do? If you're starting out in your career or in a position to change careers, prioritize flexibility in your job search. You should look for jobs and a career where you can work remotely or have significant vacation time. Even if it means a paycheck reduction, these perks are more closely tied to your goals in life and ultimately will make you happier in the long run.

You should also set your own boundaries. Technology makes you constantly accessible, nobody will set boundaries for when you should stop working, you have to set the boundaries yourself. Setting boundaries also means communicating those boundaries to those you work with.

Next, just because you see your job as secondary to your personal life doesn't mean work shouldn't be enjoyable. You'll spend at least a third of your waking hours at your job, so you might as well like what you're doing. Maybe you find out you like thinking about strategy or working with numbers. Maybe you feel invigorated by counseling and mentoring people. Once you know what gets you excited, look for assignments or projects aligned to those interests such as managing the budget or starting a mentoring program.

For others, work is a game. Winning means moving up the corporate ladder. These people accept that they will have to stay up late working on a project and make sacrifices in their personal life, but what they do not accept is not being recognized for their efforts. They get frustrated when they don't believe they are getting promoted fast enough, making enough money or getting the recognition they deserve. They have high expectations for themselves and they get especially upset when they see other people moving faster.

So what would I tell someone like this? Technology has trained you to expect instant gratification. Services such as Netflix and Amazon Prime instantly cater to your every need. Your career is one area in life where you can't get immediate results. No matter the industry, career progression takes time, effort, setbacks and awkward coworker small talk.

So if you're ambitious like this, you need to be patient. Stop creating unrealistic expectations for yourself based on who you see around you. Nobody's life is that put together. Rather than focusing on getting that next job or promotion, focus on the present. Master your current job and reflect on who you are and what you enjoy doing. Focusing on your career is fine for now, but eventually extrinsic motivators such as status and money won't be enough to satisfy and fulfill you. By truly knowing yourself, you can figure out what you really want in life and out of your career.

Ambitious high-achievers like this have a to-do list a mile long and secretly get a lot of satisfaction each time they get to scratch something off of it. When you spend all night finishing a report, the praise from your team members can be addicting. The work is always on your phone and your laptop is never too far away. You have to consciously choose not to work if you are the ambitious one like this, because it's very easy to prioritize work above everything else including your friends, family, hobbies and even your health.

You also need to take breaks. Even though breaks seem like a waste of time, they're actually productive. Daily breaks throughout the day have been shown to help maintain your quality of work. Vacations have also been shown to make you more productive because they force you to prioritize what needs to be done.

No matter who you are and where you fit on this spectrum, figure out what you want in life, figure out how more work-life balance fits into your goals, then work to make that balance happen. Just keep in mind that there will always be more work to do but you will only have one life to live. As long as you are defining the life that you want and chasing after it, you will eventually find the balance that you need.

23

BECOMING THE ULTIMATE YOU!

DO YOU EVER FEEL as though you have all this untapped potential being wasted? That you just know you've got what it takes to achieve your dreams, but for one reason or another, you feel your potential is being throttled. You may know what to do to unleash your potential, but still nothing happens. For some reason there's just not much forward movement. Something is keeping you sidelined and stuck, living your normal life while your dreams are in standby mode.

Deep down in your gut, you feel that it's finally time to make the change. It's time to upgrade to a better version of yourself. This new version is the one that will help you achieve all the things you want in life including all your hopes, dreams and desires. It will help you tap into your full unrealized potential. It will help you maximize your life and streamline the actions needed to achieve to get you to your ultimate self.

Becoming The ULTIMATE YOU seems simple on the surface. Taking massive and consistent action, moving toward your goals should do it.

Well, that's a big part of the puzzle, but it's not the entire picture. Key pieces are missing that you will need to bring together to maximize how you work toward your goals. To find those pieces, you will need to go through an exploratory self-assessment process that my online clarity course will be a guide for you on your journey of self-discovery and becoming The ULTIMATE YOU. (www.marlongrigsby.com)

Becoming The ULTIMATE YOU means getting more out of yourself in every life situation. It means doing more in less time and achieving better results. Yes, it is all about the results you get in life. However, to attain higher level results, you need to first upgrade yourself.

The objective is to upgrade yourself over the next 60 days. You can do this by assessing where you are, figuring out where you want to be and drawing up a plan of action to take you from point A to point B or from mediocrity to exemplary.

Maybe, you feel as though you're capable of climbing the career ladder and getting that promotion you've been longing for all these years. Maybe you feel as though you can take your business to another level. Maybe it's your family, your finances or your love life. Whatever it is for you, it's now time to be honest with yourself and lay down a path to help improve your life.

You can start by asking yourself some specific questions. Questions like where are you in your life right now? What goals would you like to achieve? How do you feel about where you're at and what you have achieved? How would you rate the quality of your life in this area? What are you doing well? Are you happy, fulfilled, and successful in this area? Where are you struggling at the moment? What do you really want that you have been trying to achieve in this area? Where do you feel as though you have more potential and ability? Why do you feel this way? How have you let yourself down in these areas? How could you potentially improve your situation? How could you learn from your past to help move you forward in a better way? How would raising your personal standards help you achieve your desired results faster?

Becoming The ULTIMATE YOU begins once you commit yourself to raising your personal standards to a higher level of personal excellence. You have what you have in your life right now because of the personal standards you have kept. If you have low standards for yourself in various situations, then it shouldn't come as a surprise that you are getting sub-par results. Raising your personal standards helps you perform at higher levels. When you raise your standards, you are no longer settling for mediocrity in your life. When you do this, you are shooting for the moon and if you miss, you will still reach the stars, but in either case you are pursuing higher-level actions that will get you much better results.

By far my favorite NFL football team is the Pittsburgh Steelers and their Coach Mike Tomlin has a motto in giant letters that they see as they go in and out of the locker room everyday. That motto is: "The Standard is the Standard". So they set a standard of excellence. A standard of winning. A standard of good sportsmanship, hardwork and the next man up mentality. The motto is self explanatory, but imagine if you set and raised your standard of excellence in your relationships. How about in your work? Even your family and the way you raise the children? All else doesn't matter because the standard is the standard. If you raise the standard you must follow it, so must everyone else that you interact with which makes everyone better.

You, of course, won't always achieve lofty standards, however, the act of trying moves you far more closer than if you had set them at average level. Raising your personal standards is, however, only a start. There are other pieces to this puzzle you must also bring together to maximize your full potential.

For starters, you will need a personal vision and mission statement for your life. This will help guide you along your journey toward your goal. Make sure, though, that your vision and mission play to your personal strengths and your core values. Everything you do must play to your strengths. Yes, you can work on improving your weaknesses, but it's your strengths that will carry you forward through life. Your weakness, no matter how hard you try, will always be a weakness to you.

Second, you need to commit yourself to continuous improvement. In other words, become a lifelong learner. Commit yourself to learning everything you can that could potentially help improve your life and the legacy you are creating.

Third, you need to cultivate a competitive spirit. You need to challenge yourself each day to push forward toward your goal. If you're not challenging yourself, then you're not growing and if you're not growing, then you certainly won't change. If you don't change, then things in your life that you want to take to that next level probably won't change either. Your circumstances will be as they've always been and you will yet again be holding yourself back from becoming The ULTIMATE YOU.

To shift to this new version of yourself, you also need to be willing to accept honest criticism and feedback. You need to use that feedback to make improvements. You should listen and make note of others feedback that you trust, but you should be your harshest critic yet. To hold yourself to your lofty standards, you need to be tougher on yourself than anyone else would be on you. The people who achieve massive success in life always hold themselves accountable for things that they can control. In fact, they continually challenge themselves to work harder, do better and to be better.

To round things off, you also need a plan of action that can help unite all these individual components together. The primary purpose of becoming this new you, is to guide you toward your life goals and your purpose. Your plan can also serve as a catalyst to help you broaden your skills, explore different opportunities and gain valuable experience towards your life goals and mission.

The process of becoming The ULTIMATE YOU never actually ends because there is always more to know, to learn and to do that can help move your life forward in a better way. All this primarily comes down to a commitment to lifelong learning. It's about having the willingness to learn, grow and develop yourself in a multitude of ways that supports your purpose and the vision for your life. This, however, takes work. It takes constant diligence and consistent action on your part to become a better version of yourself today than you were yesterday. It's about raising your game each and every day. It's about being better and doing better. It's about a never-ending growth and development mindset. It's about taking your life to the next level of fullfillment and success.

ACHIEVING YOUR GOALS

Achieving your goals can be difficult. We all know the routine, we set specific goals and start pushing, trying to break free from our comfort zones. Then life happens. We get distracted. Frustrated. Fed up. Overwhelmed. Eventually, we revert back to our old ways of doing things. Sound familiar?

Clearly, you have struggled with goals at some point in your life, but there are also those goals that you seem to set and achieve. In fact, nothing can deter you towards these goals. You have a determined spirit and a relentless drive, overcoming anything that stands in your way. So what's the difference between goals you eventually achieve and goals that you give up on? How can you set goals so that you can achieve them all the time and not just some times?

You are wired to want more, be more and achieve more. What you typically lose sight of is your incredible ability to rapidly manifest what you desire. As someone who helps high-achievers reach the next level of success in their lives and businesses, knowing the proper strategies is extremely important. The individuals who make the biggest impacts, have what I call, the high-performance mindset. How would you feel knowing that if you followed a few simple steps, you could literally achieve anything you desired in any area of your life? Here's the formula on what you need to do.

Get crystal clear on what you want. So many people never achieve what they desire simply because they are never completely sure on what they actually want. In order to rapidly manifest your desires, you need to get clear on exactly what it is that you want in your life. I'm not talking about a broad goal setting here. I'm talking about being crystal clear on every detail associated with what it is that you desire.

Ask yourself right now, once you achieve this goal, what will it specifically look like in your life? What will it feel like? How will it change your life? How will it affect the decisions you make? Be as specific as possible here, as I want you to be able to see and feel what the future will be like once accomplished. Write down what you want to bring into existence. This may seem like a lot of hard work, but trust me, it works. Sit down and write out exactly what you want in life. The key is that you need to write out exactly what you desire as if it has already happened. The reasoning for this is rather simple. Your unconscious mind does not know the difference between your dreams and realities. So, the faster you can convince your subconscious that the desired result has already manifested, the faster it will show up in your reality.

You need to stop worrying about the "how". This is the step that will make or break your manifestation of your dreams. Let go of "how" because if you don't, you won't be able to create the space for what you desire to show up in your life. By human nature, you are wired to plan and want everything to happen specifically to that plan, however, this limits everything to flow as it should into your life. The key is to focus on the end result and to be open to however it will manifest, rather than needing it to look a specific way.

You will also have to learn to create a massive emotional connection to you and your dreams. Every high performer knows and understands that the event with the highest emotional connection is what will show up in your life. You need to start tapping into this emotional peak state whenever you are thinking about what you desire to manifest and achieve in your life.

When you are writing out exactly what you desire, allow yourself to tap into the feeling associated with you achieving or receiving that dream. Notice how good it feels. Double that feeling. Triple that feeling. Make a conscious effort to tap into that feeling as regularly as possible throughout the day. Ensure that you are not consumed with negative thoughts and emotions throughout your day, otherwise, you will simply manifest more of those negative experiences.

Obsess over your goals daily. This last step is crucial. Once you are crystal clear about what goals you desire, you have to write them into existence with your heart and your mind. Let go of how it is going to happen and develop a strong emotional connection. Obsess about it daily.

Connecting emotionally with what you want to create once a day isn't going to cut it. You need to connect emotionally several times a day to ensure you don't lose your focus or that emotional connection. Your goals will have no option but to come true. A great way to do this is to set an alarm for various times throughout the day that you allow yourself to tap into the emotion of having already accomplished your goals. This will allow everything you desire to naturally show up with ease and things will just flow.

Some of the insights here may seem rather unusual, but if you give them a try, I'm confident you'll see the achievement you want. Remember, having a high-performance mindset simply takes time and consistency. I encourage you to try it for 30 days and just see where it takes you. You're going to like the change you get and what you are able to accomplish once you give it a chance. Setting goals is a great tool to help you achieve your desired success. It's easy to start off strong and with enthusiasm, but that fades with time and setbacks. Whether your goals are large or small, there are usually a few key reasons why you're struggling to achieve them. You either give up too soon, take criticism personally, rather than productively, you lack consistency or you don't have a solid plan.

There is very little chance of achieving your goals without strategic planning. Goal achievement requires ample planning so that you know what direction you need to go in. This doesn't mean you need to know every single action you'll have to take. Think about an airplane for a moment. An airplane has a goal of taking off and landing in a specific city, on a specific date and at a specific time. In order to achieve that goal, the plane needs to make a plan, also known as its flight plan, but that flight plan can change. At the outset, it accounts for some averages, such as average speed, average altitude and general course of travel. Other things can and do change along the way due to air traffic congestion, turbulence, weather and other factors. So the plane needs to adjust its plan accordingly. Similarly, you need to create a plan that you can stick to, but then adjust along the way towards achieving your goals. Don't change the goal, but you can and should change the plan as often as needed to get closer to your goals.

No goal of yours can be achieved without personal discipline. Even if you write out your goals and set them the right way, without discipline, following through becomes next to impossible. Create an atmosphere for goal achievement by instituting the right habits into your life that will foster the discipline required for success. To be disciplined, you need order and organization. When things are chaotic and you're losing your grip on things, it's far harder to stay focused on achieving your goals, but order and organization leads to better discipline, which in turn leads to a higher percentage of goal achievement.

Often, your obligations can outpace your actions but, for the person that can organize their chaotic life, discipline is just around the corner. It's also very easy to get distracted in life. You have things that pull you in multiple directions. You veer off course, moving to one tangent after another which lessens the likelihood of you achieving your goals. You need to minimize the distractions in your life so that you can remain focused. Take a good look at where your distractions are coming from and work to eliminate the ones that suck up a majority of your time. This includes excessive socializing, Netflix & chilling, social media and any other time-wasters. By removing the distractions, you then have more free time to pursue your goals rather than focusing on the things that don't matter as much. It's probably no surprise to where much of your free time is going already and what distractions are eating away at your schedule, so do your best to eliminate those.

Milestones are helpful markers that you can create in route to your goals. Simply take your long-term goal of one or more years and break that goal into specific milestones along the way. Create monthly and weekly milestones that will help you stay on track. If you actually created a measurable goal, then creating milestones is very easy, just break them up into equal parts. For example, to lose 60 pounds within 1 year, you need to lose 5 pounds per month or 1.25 pounds per week. Milestones are far more manageable because it helps you see the short-term results that will lead you to your long-term outcome. It's more finite, manageable and encouraging on a day-to-day basis, since the long-term goals can often times be overwhelming.

Procrastination is the silent killer to your goals and dreams. It affects everyone near and far. Letting procrastination overcome you can result in a slow and steady goal-achievement death. It's easy to allow your natural tendencies to put things off for later and this can become habitual patterns that you don't want. You have to do what it takes to rid procrastination from your life. You can't achieve big goals with procrastination looming. If you have a tendency to procrastinate, then you need to implement some strategies for taking back control of your life and your schedule. Start with the 15-minute rule. Set a timer on your phone and dedicate yourself to doing something for 15 minutes that you've been putting off. Why 15 minutes? It helps build momentum. It moves you in the direction that you're after by only promising a small commitment to yourself, but what you'll find is that after those 15 minutes are up, you'll keep going, as any object in motion tends to stay in motion. Give it a try, it works. As you master 15-minute increments with no distraction, bump it up to 20-minutes, 30-minutes, etc.

Time management is also a strategy that anyone can use to achieve their goals faster. In fact, this single strategy, if implemented well, can help anyone achieve even the most lofty goals. Find a good system that works for you to manage your time and implement it. Time management helps you to avoid distractions while also utilizing the one thing that everyone has in common, time. No one person in the world has more time than the other. Time is the great equalizer across the planet. So, how do you use yours? Do you spend it the right way, ensuring that you're allocating a good amount of time towards achieving your goals across all of your different life area goals or do you squander it away? Be open and honest with yourself when implementing a system to make sure that it works best for you.

Your MITs, or your "Most Important Tasks" of the day, are those things that you can do today to move you closer to your long-term goals. Mark Twain called these tasks "frogs" and is famous for saying that "If it's your job to eat a frog, it's best to do it first thing in the morning. And If it's your job to eat two frogs, it's best to eat the biggest one first." Twain was referring to the MITs that you have in a given day. Focus your morning ritual on tackling your MITs first and watch your progress towards your goals take enormous leaps forward, faster than you ever thought was possible.

Another methodology is the 80/20-Rule, also known as the Pareto Principle, which states that 80% of your results come from 20% of your actions. In sales, this also means that 80% of the sales comes from 20% of the clients. It's your job to identify the 20% of your actions that will produce 80% of your results, then compound on those efforts. To identify your 80/20, you need to audit your activities related to your goals. What efforts are you putting in and what outcomes are you receiving from those efforts? Of course, the only way to ensure you determine this properly is by constantly measuring your results on a daily basis. This isn't a simple procedure since we're such creatures of habit, but when you can find your 80/20 in life, you can really take your results to the next level.

Failure is common when trying to achieve your goals. The biggest part about failure is that you often don't anticipate it. So, when you do fail, it's far harder to deal with, but when you anticipate failure, you can better cope with it and adjust your plans accordingly. The most successful people in the world have failed many times. You can anticipate failure along your journey and you should use it as stepping-stones, not allowing them to kill your spirit as you work to achieve your future goals and life dreams, but as what it is, a learning lesson in the wrong way to do something.

25

OVERCOMING OBSTACLES IN YOUR WAY

WHEN CONFRONTED WITH LIFE'S obstacles, it's easy to become overwhelmed, however, no matter what life throws your way, keep in mind that you always have options. There are always things you can do, actions you can take and decisions you can make that will help keep you focused and on track with your goals. Here are some ideas to help you overcome some of life's toughest obstacles.

It's easy to think that truly successful people were just more fortunate people from birth. They had the talent, the looks, the money, everything they needed to succeed and to some extent, it may be true. Those from stable families who were not burdened by poverty or physical limitations do have it easier than those who have major obstacles to overcome, but there are countless examples of people who have reached unparalleled success despite significant challenges in their lives. In fact, it could be that those very limitations propelled them to strive for heights they may not have reached for otherwise. Whatever the reasons for their success, these are people who can inspire you to accomplish your goals despite any of your own specific obstacles.

The next time that you are tempted to give up in the face of a formidable obstacle, consider that Benjamin Franklin couldn't afford to attend school after he turned 10. Oprah Winfrey was abused as a child and ran away from home at age 13. Franklin D. Roosevelt lost the use of his legs to polio before becoming president. Vincent van Gogh is believed to have suffered from bipolar disorder. Helen Keller became deaf and blind when she was 18 months old. Beethoven suffered from tinnitus and a gradual loss of hearing. Winston Churchill had dyslexia and suffered emotional instability. Walt Disney had attention deficit disorder and the list goes on and on.

Many of these accomplished people would likely say they gained useful character traits as a result of their particular obstacles, which ultimately aided them in their success. Their individual stories can be an inspiration for all those dealing with their own challenges. So let's take a look at some strategies that successful people have used to overcome physical, mental and financial obstacles.

Whatever you do, don't give up! This is probably the one common characteristic of all successful people and it is an especially important trait for anyone struggling with a disability or other challenge. The inventor of the light bulb and the phonograph, Thomas Edison, is well known for his relentless perseverance. It is said that Edison tried thousands of ways to develop the electric light bulb until he finally succeeded. "Why, I have not failed," he once explained, "I've just found 10,000 ways that won't work." Edison also overcame his own childhood obstacles, he suffered from hearing loss and was labeled "as unable to think clearly" by his teacher so his mother home schooled him.

You should also not make comparisons to others. It is natural for people to compare themselves to others and feel inferior as a result. Such comparisons, can be very self-defeating. Others may seem richer, smarter or better looking and being compared to them can be demotivating. Successful people believe in their own self-worth, despite what others may present as evidence to the contrary. If you tend to compare yourself negatively to others, I implore you to celebrate what makes you different and focus on your many positive attributes. As Steve Jobs once said, "your time is limited, so don't waste it living someone else's life."

You should also stay positive. Physical conditions, disabilities and any other perceived weaknesses can cloud your perspective on life. Those who effectively overcome difficulties are good at putting their conditions into perspective. Whatever the obstacle, it is just one area of life. It's okay to be sad, disappointed or angry at the problem, but positive people are also grateful for what they do have and they don't lose hope for the future. It's natural to focus on the negative, but be encouraged to make an effort to cultivate a positive attitude. This type of positivity can be empowering and it can prevent the negative feelings from taking over and causing you to fall into a depression.

People who have overcome life's obstacles have also found new ways to look at old problems. In order to overcome their own difficulties, they have had to think creatively, a skill which makes them successful in other areas of their lives too. The old saying that refers to challenges as opportunities is very true. Successful people are not afraid to fail as they try new solutions. They just look for ways to overcome the obstacle that is in their path. Remember that failure is a part of life and many people who are undeniably successful have often failed publicly. "I've missed more than 9,000 shots in my career," NBA G.O.A.T. Michael Jordan is quoted as saying. "I've lost almost 300 games. 26 times, I've been trusted to take the game winning shot and missed. I've failed over and over and over again in my life. And that is why I succeed."

People who overcome challenges also use the S.M.A.R.T. (smart, measurable, attainable, realistic, and timely) technique to set achievable, yet still, challenging goals. Then they track progress and make adjustments along the way, if necessary. Successful people have an end in sight and they work hard to get there. Actor Jim Carrey, who had to overcome dyslexia and the trauma of being homeless for a time as a child, wrote himself a check for $10 million for "acting services rendered", post-dating it to ten years in the future. Keeping this check in his wallet allowed him to visualize his goal of one day becoming a successful actor. Do you know what happened exactly ten years later? He did a little movie called "Dumb & Dumber" where he was paid $10 million dollars as the principle actor! I tell you that story to tell you to hold on to your dreams no matter what. Many challenges in life may seem insurmountable and limiting, but people throughout history have proven that obstacles can be overcome and can even be beneficial for you. A drawback may be a setup for a come back.

Finally, no matter what, do not quit, because the greatest opportunities are always intertwined with life's most significant struggles. Persistence and perseverance, a commitment to consistency and massive action are what you need to overcome your life's biggest obstacles, no matter how big you think they are.

Obstacles are just "things" that are there to teach and strengthen you for the journey that lies ahead. You must, therefore, not view them as insurmountable problems that are preventing you from achieving your goals, but rather as small and at times significant, stepping stones that are required "modules" that you need to pass through to obtain your MBA for real life success. Take the time to learn the lessons that life throws your way. These lessons will be critical to your success as you make progress along your journey to becoming The ULTIMATE YOU.

26

SIMPLICITY AS A BLUEPRINT FOR SUCCESS

MODERN LIFE CAN BE overwhelming. You have screens in front of you all day from your phone, to your computer, to your TVs. You're now connected to the rest of the world 24/7. This is great, but it also has its disadvantages.

Today most people spend so much time looking at screens instead of looking at actual people. Society as a whole put so much focus on building virtual friends instead of nurturing a group of close friends in real life. Technology has made you so fanatical about trying to keep up with a million things at once that your productivity drops, your mind never truly rests and you gradually build up stress over everything going on in the world and with you. This on top of our obsession over material items, is the major reason your life has become unnecessarily complicated. You connect happiness to getting the next new gadget or thing to the point where, unless you get it, your mind is never at peace. When you do get it, the satisfying feeling quickly dissipates like sand sifting through your hands. Then, you're off to acquire something else to get that feeling back. This cycle of consumption never results in peace. It never brings you to true happiness, but mostly stress, anxiety, anger and frustration.

By shedding your need for more, simplifying your life and accepting the present moment as it is, you cultivate the ground for true happiness. Happiness is not built upon outside forces, but upon your own inner peace.

At its essence, simplifying your life is about removing distractions. It's about finding peace in the margin you create for yourself by removing distractions and mindfully choosing where to place your time. Whether it's your job, children, wife or husband, mother or father, your faith or whomever or whatever is most important to you, that's where you should funnel your time.

There are many ways to remove distractions and simplify your life if you only take a second to look around. Once you start reducing and decluttering, you'll not only have room to breathe but more time to spend doing what's most important to you. A simple life has a different meaning and a different value for every person.

For me, it means eliminating all but the essentials, trading in chaos for peace and spending my time doing what's most important to me. It means getting rid of many of the things I occupy my time with so I can spend time with people I love and do the things that I like to do. It means getting rid of the clutter so that I'm left with only things which provide me some sort of value. However, getting to this kind of life simplicity isn't always a simple process. It's a journey, not a destination, and it can often be two steps forward and one step backward.

If you've been feeling weighed down, rather than trying to find ways to make it all work, consider looking for things you can remove from your life. With a few subtle changes, you might be surprised by how much more time you now have on your hands.

You can also try getting rid of the unncessary stuff. Most people have much more than they actually need. Despite this, a good sale or cool item may inspire you to add to our collection. In so many ways, society reinforces this belief that possessions will make you happy and will impress the people around you. This focus on the material things keeps your mind and your home cluttered. For example, there are probably things in your closet that you haven't worn or thought about in years, that should be donated to your local Goodwill, no matter how "nice" it is or if you may "need" it one day.

You can also get rid of unhelpful people. Relationships are complex and require a significant investment of time. When everyone is putting in the time and effort, it's often worth the trouble, but if someone is draining your energy and adding nothing but negativity to your life, you may need to reevaluate that relationship.

Another key thing to do, especially if you have fitness goals or finanical goals, is to start meal planning. Most of us can relate to that sinking feeling at the end of the day when you're not sure what to eat for dinner. You wonder if whatever you have in your fridge or pantry is enough to throw together a meal but, too often you just end up hitting a drive-thru or ordering take out. At first, meal planning can seem like a bit of a chore, but over time it will save you both time and money. Come up with a list of things that are easy to cook and tasty. On Sunday, pick up everything you need for the week and then assign each meal its own day. Stick with it and after a couple weeks, you will see how much easier it is to have a meal plan and not having to run to the grocery every other day will save you time.

You can also create a morning ritual to follow. It's tempting to hit that snooze button a few times when your alarm goes off. An alternative is to create a ritual that gets your morning off to a more positive start. The night before, lay out your clothes, pack your bag and then go to bed at a reasonable time. Set your alarm for half an hour earlier than you need so that you can do something that makes you feel good such as reading, praying, excercise, yoga, stretching, a short walk, work on your MIT or sipping a hot beverage by a window. Make the choice to do this every morning and reap the benefits throughout the day.

A hard one for most, myself included, is to unplug from technology. We are so tethered to our devices that it's hard to believe we survived before they were invented. While it's not realistic to go off the grid entirely, you can make a conscious effort to unplug when it's not needed, especially at bedtime. Try leaving your phone in airplane mode during dinner or turning off the television in favor of playing a board game with your family. Reconnect with yourself and others by being present in the moment, without being pulled into notifications from a hundred different apps all trying to capture your time and attention.

You can take unplugging from tech a little further and deactivate your social media accounts. If you ever complain that you don't have enough time to do all that you need to do in a day, please count how much time is wasted by staring at one of your many screens. It doesn't have to be permanent but deactivating social media, even for just a few short days, can help remind you of what's truly important. Once you get past the uncomfortable feeling of not being "connected" and like you are going to miss something important, you will be stunned by how much time you gain by doing this. If deactivating is not something you feel you can do, try doing what they did on the Nissan Altima commercial "Be There", where the man in the commerical gets a text and then gets in his car and drives across town and gets to his friends house and says, "nothing much, how about you". His friend then proceeds to say, "are you answering my text in-person?" Such a novel idea. Spend some face-to-face time with your friends instead of sharing your life from behind the screen and calling it social.

Is your life organized? It can be time consuming to go through and organize all the different areas of your life, but it's better than wasting time trying to find the shoes you need to wear or the bills you need to pay. Instead of wasting another panicked minute tracking down lost items, come up with a better system. As soon as you're finished using something, put it back where it belongs. That way, everything will always be where it's supposed to be when you need it. If need be, pick up some bins, folders or containers to help you tame the madness. It will feel so good knowing where everything is at all times.

If organizing your life is too difficult, maybe you should consider downsizing in every way. It's much easier to be organized and prepared when you are a minimalist. As I mentioned, we all tend to have more things around us than we actually need. Downsizing can really simplify your life so that you can focus your attention on what really matters. In addition to shedding possessions and ending relationships that no longer serve you, it may also be helpful to reduce your number of commitments. If you're struggling with running kids around and following their social calendars or maybe even you have too many activities on yours. Whatever the case, learn to start saying no and leaving some margin and time for you. While it's great to give back and also spend time with friends, it's also important to have boundaries.

Fininacial margin is another great thing to get for simplicity. Whether it's a mortgage, student loans, a car payment or a credit card balance, most people owe some sort of debt. Many will bury their heads in the sand, unaware of how much they really owe or how long it will take to repay it. There's this mentality that some use that if you do the minimum and pretend it's not there, it will go away, but it won't. Challenge yourself to get up close and personal with your debt. Instead of ignoring your financial problems, face them head on. It will feel great to have one less thing to worry about.

In today's materialistic world, you might get fooled into the belief that having more will make you happy. While that might be true for a select few, the reality is that for most, you already have way more than you need, no matter how much you think you don't have. I once heard a pastor say that if your car has a home, meaning a garage, you are rich compared to 75% of the rest of the world. So, think about making a conscious decision to simplify your life by whittling down your possessions, commitments and the people in it. Address any nagging worries, doubts and regrets while focusing on personal goals and authentic sources of happiness. By decluttering your life, you open up space for the things that are truly important. Rather than filling up every corner of your home or moment on your schedule, find happiness in personal growth and fulfillment. Embrace a simplified life and you will gain much more than you ever dreamed. In summary, if I was to narrow it down to two steps to simplifying for success as you become The ULTIMATE YOU, I would do the following:

1. Identify what's most important to you.
2. Eliminate everything else.

27

LIVE YOUR LEGACY

WHAT'S YOUR LEGACY? WHAT do you want to be remembered for? How do you want to be remembered by your family, your friends and others? A legacy is not a quantifiable substance. Building a legacy that lasts doesn't involve following any single path or making a particular-sized pledge, but there are elements shared by every successful person who's left a legacy.

As the famous proverb goes, "this too shall pass". You only live for a brief moment in time. Even when you feel being stuck in some bad situation forever, life will change for the better. This change is inevitable and it's up to you how long the change will take and if it is a change for the better or the worse.

So how do you want people to remember you? Do you live just for yourself or do you want to leave a legacy that will inspire others? It's super easy to get stuck in little things just like hurrying, being busy or in petty arguments. You can lose your direction in life when you lack clarity about who you are and what you want to express in your life.

It's more rewarding to broaden your perspective, stop feeling so important and stop taking situations and people for granted. How do you want your loved ones to remember you? What is your legacy going to be? Living your legacy doesn't need to be anything special or memorable. It's about your own energy, how you make others feel and what you teach them through your everyday life.

Having a life vision greater than you will give you strength whenever you need it. Your life is not just about you but it's about the impact that you will have on others, so make it a positive one. Living your legacy doesn't deprive you from hardships and struggles, but it'll get you through them. Lowering your own self-importance and being humble helps you to not get defeated by life challenges so easily. Not everything is about you, sometimes, compassion can teach you more than a thousand words.

Without knowing why you're here, the puprose you have, you will drift into the wind aimlessly, like a sailboat with no rutter. Living your legacy gives you the solid ground that lets you live a life in accordance with the best version of yourself. By bringing integrity into your life, you make it much easier for yourself and others. Integrity creates stability in your thoughts and feelings. You don't get influenced by the opinions of others and you're able to say no when needed without hesitation. You take full ownership of your choices and decisions thus growing into a fully mature person.

Living your legacy brings clarity into your life when you know exactly what you want to create. You don't let others influence you negatively because you know your value, your worth and your calling. Imagine how much time and energy you can save by knowing how you want to create your life.

When you're faced with two options, it's simpler to decide what is in accordance with your legacy and what is just a mere distraction. People and situations try to hook you so you will give them your attention, time and energy. These are three of the most valuable assets you have to play in this game called life. Don't give them away thoughtlessly. The time that has passed cannot be undone or returned. If you feel like you're wasting your life then you may become more mindful about where you are putting your energy.

Finally, there is nothing more fulfilling than living a life in accordance with your inner values. When you do this, you tap into a deeper meaning of your life. I don't know anyone who would live their legacy and life's purpose, but at the same time not feel fulfilled. These two conditions don't exist in the same universe. It's like oil and water, they just don't mix. So what is your legacy going to say about you? Hopefully, it will say, you lived life as The ULTIMATE YOU!

28

CONCLUSION

WELL, CONGRATULATIONS, YOU DID it! You are now one step closer to getting everything you ever wanted in life. See, becoming The ULTIMATE YOU is not about arriving in life. It's not some complicated formula to get ahead. It's simply about learning the life principles to be you, but only better. An upgraded version of yourself, if you will. It's like the latest software update for your life, but with all the new bells and whistles as new features for you to become the best you possible.

The ULTIMATE YOU is about learning to embrace yourself, align with your vision and build the habits and skills to make your dream life a reality. This will allow you to embrace your true potential and live your best life possible.

As you have seen, there is nothing in this book that is rocket science. Probably not even a new concept that was just so mind blowing. Maybe not even something you haven't heard before. However, when you put all these life behaviors, principles and values together, it makes you a much better person. Many times you go through life without intentionality and purpose. You get so busy and wrapped up in the heavy responsibilities of home and work, you forget about yourself. It is my hope and prayer that you are able to take these life principals and weave them into your life for better understanding on how to live your life, with more clarity and more on fire than ever before.

Through this book you have learned many life concepts that will set you up for success, however, there is still so much more work to do. I encourage you to take these concepts a step further and invest in yourself through The ULTIMATE YOU clarity course. This course is designed to take all the principles in this book and to have practical application in your life and to apply them immediately. If you stick with me and do the work you will upgrade yourself and take your life to that next level in 60 days! To learn more go to (www.marlongrigsby.com).

This clarity course will help you get the life clarity that is still needed for you and we will create a full action plan for your life. By following this life plan, it will allow you to take life by its horns and stop letting it just happen to you, but you start happening to it. You will begin to start to live your legacy. That legacy that you always wanted, including achieving all your hopes, dreams and desires.

Can you imagine if you started living this way, with crystal clear clarity. Knowing what you needed to be doing at all times and how you need to react in specific situations with confidence. No matter what life throws at you, with clarity, it doesn't detour you off your path of greatness. That's what becoming The ULTIMATE YOU is all about and that's where you are on your way to living life.

As we depart, I want to leave you with a mentality as you become The ULTIMATE YOU. The death of the legendary and iconic Kobe Bryant in 2020 took the world by surprise. There have been certain untimely deaths in my lifetime that I have had emotional connections to that will forever be etched in my brain. The passing of Tupac, Biggie and Aaliyah all stand out for me. Kobe, on the other hand, is that once in a lifetime event that crosses all cultures, ethnicities, social economics, sports fans and non-fans alike. I guess this is what it was like in my parents' lifetime when John F. Kennedy and Martin Luther King Jr. were assassinated.

Some events are just too hard to believe, especially given Kobe Bryant's seemingly invincible persona. On Sunday, Jan. 26, 2020, the world stood still as news of Kobe's death began hitting the internet. Kobe Bryant and his 13-year-old daughter, Gianna Bryant and seven others were killed in a helicopter crash on the way to a basketball game at the Mamba Academy in California.

This day was a devastating day for not only the families involved, but for sports fans everywhere. Whether you had a personal connection to the "Black Mamba," idolized him as a child or were just a casual fan, millions across the globe stopped and mourned the loss of an icon. People gathered outside the Staples Center, Kobe's homecourt for his entire 20-year career with tears in their eyes and flowers in their arms. Expressions of pure shock and profound sadness inscribed across each face.

How could one man, one person, have such a global impact? I would say he truly lived his legacy. He had become The ULTIMATE YOU for himself.

Throughout his 20-year NBA career, Kobe's basketball prowess earned him 18 All-Star selections, 5 NBA championship titles, 2 NBA Finals MVP awards and 2 Olympic gold medals. He was one of the greatest pure scorers basketball has ever seen, ranking third on the all-time scoring list before LeBron James passed him not even 24 hours before his death. His 81-point game against the Raptors is the second-most points ever scored in an NBA game by one person. Off the court, Bryant was a published author, philanthropist, partner of a venture capital firm, head of his own media studio, husband and a dedicated father to four girls.

Though Kobe did possess heaps of raw talent, his fellow professional athletes contend it was his sheer mental fortitude that propelled him to greatness. He was so much more than his Hall-of-Fame numbers. He was a way of life. His famous "Mamba Mentality," a relentless work ethic, will be his lasting mark on the world. He knew how to push himself, no matter what he was doing, to be the absolute best that he could be. He spent countless hours in the gym, perfecting his game to the point where we recognized him as basketball royalty.

Mamba Mentality goes beyond basketball. It's applicable to everyone, you included. You want to be the best engineer? Well, put in the work. You want to be the best journalist? Put in the work. You want to be the best parent or spouse you can be? Put in the work.

When asked about how he defined the Mamba Mentality, Kobe said this. "To be on a constant quest to try to be the best version of yourself. That's what the mentality is. It's not a finite thing. It's a constant quest to try to be better today than you were yesterday and better tomorrow than you were the day before." It is a never-ending cycle.

The relentless effort to pursue greatness will be Kobe's everlasting impact on the world. Sure, he was one of the most decorated athletes to walk the earth, but that can't be passed on.

Around 2003-2004, Kobe was at a low point in his career and personal life, so he decided to do something unusual, he created an alter-ego. Thus, "The Black Mamba" was born. The particular name was chosen after Kobe saw Kill Bill, in which an assassin kills another character with a venomous snake. Kobe remarked on the nature of the snake's length, bite, strike, and temperament and was captivated by the way snakes shed their skin, which was a reference to growing out of his old self.

If you want to be great in a particular area, you have to obsess over it. A lot of people say they want to be great, but they're not willing to make the sacrifices necessary to achieve greatness. They have other concerns, whether important or not and they spread themselves out way too thin.

Everyone who ever played with Kobe knows that he was always the first one to show up at practice, sometimes injured and often before the lights even came on. Sometimes five hours before practice even started. He once warmed up before a practice from 4:15 a.m. to 11 a.m., refusing to leave until he made 800 shots. Even in high school, Kobe would practice from 5 a.m. until 7 a.m., before classes started. He would also challenge his high school teammates to one-on-one games, first to 100. He won his first game 100-12.

Off the court, Kobe was just as obsessive. He cold-called and texted numerous business people and entrepreneurs to pick their brains about business success, sometimes at 3 a.m. He started his own media company dedicated to storytelling and produced a short-animated documentary that won an Oscar. He taught himself to play Beethoven's

"Moonlight Sonata" by ear on the piano. There's no denying he was hyper-focused in his pursuit of greatness.

In addition to mastery, you must accept failure as part of the learning process. Failure is inevitable, and when done the right way, it has a lot to teach us about improvement. Kobe said "If I wanted to implement something new into my game, I'd see it and try incorporating it immediately. I wasn't scared of missing, looking bad, or being embarrassed. That's because I always kept the end result, the long game, in my mind. I always focused on the fact that I had to try something to get it, and once I got it, I'd have another tool in my arsenal. If the price was a lot of work and a few missed shots, I was okay with that."

Kobe realized and so should you, that if you want to improve or learn something new, you're going to fail at your first attempts. But through repetition and trials, you will eventually improve. When you understand that failure is an integral tool for bettering yourself, then you no longer need to be afraid. That's an important thing to keep in mind. What inhibits many from achieving or even pursuing their goals they say they want is the fear of failure or embarrassing themself in front of others.

The Mamba Mentality has been adopted by hundreds and thousands of athletes and others around the world. His daughter Gigi was known as "Mambacita" because she was so much like her father. She put in the work to be one of the best young basketball players in the country, pursuing her dream of one day becoming a UConn Husky. Though the dream was taken away far too quickly, the mentality remains.

So, as you strive to become The Ultimate YOU, I implore you to embrace the mentality of the Mamba. No matter who you are, where you're from or what you do, strive to be better. Work every day to be the best you that you can be. Wake up early. Go to bed late. Do what it takes to achieve your greatness.

That's how the Mamba lived. Kobe and Gigi may be gone, but their legacy can live in all of us. This is what living your legacy means. This is what becoming The Ultimate YOU means.

Think about what Kobe tried to impart. What areas in your life could you apply this? Are there certain things you're good at that you could become a master of? Are you putting in the work necessary to achieve mastery? Are you letting the fear of failure inhibit your pursuit of success? Kobe understood that success was the result of putting in the reps. Which basically means, we are what we repeatedly do. Excellence, then, is not an act, but a habit.

My company is for the high-achievers, the passionate, the fearless and the dreamers who believe. It is for those who are smart, curious and conscious with an open mind, a drive for learning, a desire for self-discovery and a deep desire to live their legacy.

My journey to this point has not been an easy one, as I have had many setbacks and yet it has been the most difficult and challenging times that have transformed me the most, for the better. I've learned that character is crafted and carved from chaos and crisis. My ability to overcome challenging obstacles with creativity and a positive attitude have made me a better man, father, friend and just all-around a better person.

Part of my life's vision is to help 1 million people through a life clarity seeking process and learn how to live their life to their fullest potential. My mission is to help others go from being stuck to being unstoppable with direction and passion to their ultimate life goals. My mission is to create products and services around simplifying life, inspiring greatness, maximizing potential, legacy building and launching other's hopes and dreams. My mission is to serve as a brace for those whose hopes have been dashed and to be a cast for those with broken dreams, as I pour into them and lead by example, as I turn their discouragement and heartache into courage and strength.

My passion is to motivate and inspire you to maximize your potential and live the life you were meant to live. I believe that true success is about discovering and fulfilling your purpose. Those I have worked with achieve refocused clarity and renewed confidence by becoming the ultimate versions of themselves. True success is about fulfilling your purpose and becoming all that you were designed to be. If you want to discover more, please explore the various ways to work with me and how you can gain the clarity to become The Ultimate YOU, via my website (www.marlongrigsby.com).

The Ultimate YOU clarity course is about knowing where you want to go and how you're going to get there. A life without purpose and meaning is like getting in your car with no destination in mind. You have zero confidence on where you are going, as if you are just going through life on cruise control, literally just wasting time until you figure life out and where you want to go.

Becoming The Ultimate YOU helps you achieve absolute success in whatever it is that you pursue. When you start to truly understand and behave within the concepts that we will go through, you will start to see your success accelerate exponentially through every aspect of your life.

Trust me. If it was possible for me, it's 100% possible for you, too! I'm not special. I'm just a person who has learned how to get myself unstuck, once and for all. Always remember no one is better at being you, than you. So make sure you are becoming The Ultimate YOU!

Made in the USA
Coppell, TX
01 March 2021